HOME DECORATING
SOURCEBOOK

Printed textile circa 1920.

HOME DECORATING
SOURCEBOOK

MARK TURNER
LESLEY HOSKINS

CRESCENT
BOOKS

First published as *Silver Studio of Design*
in Great Britain 1988 by
Webb & Bower (Publishers) Limited
in association with Michael Joseph Limited

This 1995 edition published by Crescent Books,
distributed by Random House Value Publishing, Inc.,
40 Engelhard Avenue
Avenel
New Jersey 07001

Random House
New York • Toronto • London • Sydney • Auckland

Designed by Peter Wrigley

Production by Nick Facer/Rob Kendrew

Text and illustrations produced in association with
Middlesex University England
© Middlesex University 1988

A CIP catalog record for this book is available from the Library of Congress

ISBN 0-517-14157-4

Typeset in Great Britain by P&M Typesetting Ltd, Exeter, Devon

Printed and bound in Singapore

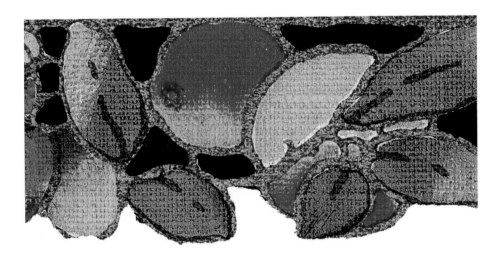

CONTENTS

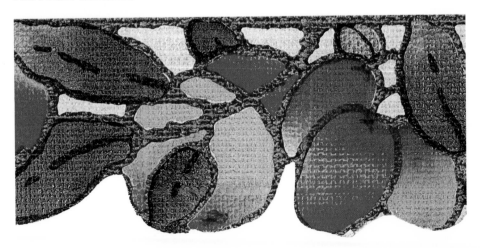

FoREWoRD

T his book is intended to show the history of the interior decoration of the small English house from 1880 to 1940. Much of the material illustrated comes from the Silver Studio Collection housed at Middlesex University, Bounds Green Road, London, N11 2NQ.

Arthur Silver, who founded the Studio in 1880, and his sons Rex and Harry were responsible for the production of many thousands of designs for the wallpapers, fabrics, linoleums and carpets which were subsequently bought by the middle-class householder. The Silvers understood middle-class decorating tastes perfectly, and worked consistently for firms who catered for both the lower end of the social scale and the more prosperous. We have deliberately avoided writing about the houses of the very poor – which during the period in question contained very little – and the houses of the rich and avant-garde, which are already well documented. However, we have tried to stress that, then as now, middle-class interiors varied greatly – the house of a humble clerk was always decorated in a very different way from that of a successful businessman.

Because the Silvers designed for such a wide range of manufacturers who in turn supplied wallpapers, textiles and floor-coverings to the entire English middle class, we can form a clear and accurate picture of the types and patterns of decoration which were available at any one time. We have also supplemented the illustrations of patterns with contemporary photographs and drawings of interiors to show clearly how the textiles and wallpapers were used and the furniture arranged.

We have divided the book into the following sections which roughly coincide with major changes in attitudes to home decoration: 1880 to 1895; 1895 to 1910; 1910 to 1925; 1925 to 1940. Changes were, of course, gradual and many factors influenced the style of house decoration – in particular education and income.

Left: Design for a wallpaper, circa 1890, by Arthur Silver. This is an excellent example of how Japanese art was influencing English pattern design at this time. The strongly aquatic flavour of this particular wallpaper pattern would indicate an intention for use in bathrooms.

INTRODUCTION

One of the great business successes of the 1970s and 80s has been Laura Ashley, whose simple early nineteenth-century sprigged chintz patterns for wallpapers and fabrics enchanted a generation brought up on bleak Modern Movement design and lugubrious reproduction William Morris in rather nasty and inaccurate colours. In the 1930s economic and political uncertainties encouraged many people to turn their houses into quite passable reproductions of Elizabethan manor houses. For similar reasons in the 1970s Laura Ashley prints and a judicious use of stripped pine furniture could make your house look like an early Victorian cottage, as different as possible from an office, a safe and welcome refuge from busy traffic and a competitive outside world. Importantly, Laura Ashley has been responsible for introducing a new generation to the idea of using accurate reproductions of historic patterns in their houses. From turning the inside of your home into an early nineteenth-century country cottage with the aid of a Laura Ashley catalogue, to considering the accurate period decoration of your house is but a short step. A great many of us live in small houses built between 1880 and 1940 and this book is intended to show how these were decorated and furnished. It is written in the hope that the readers will be encouraged to put some of the decorative schemes into practice, and manufacturers of wallpapers and fabrics inspired to reproduce appropriate designs.

In the United States great progress has been made in this direction with the aid of the invaluable *Old House Journal* – a magazine which I cannot praise too highly for the integrity and accuracy of its articles, be it on repairing a Queen-Anne Revival porch or restoring the kitchen linoleum in a 1920s bungalow. In England we are becoming rather good at the sensitive decoration and restoration of small nineteenth-century houses – though there is still much scope for improvement. We continue, however, to commit appalling acts of vandalism on the post 1900 house both inside and out. In particular, our treatment of the surburban villa of the 1920s and 30s is quite shocking. It is not often appreciated that these houses are an important development in the English vernacular tradition and should be cherished as such. We are showing numerous illustrations of decorative schemes for these houses which were originally decorated and furnished in a particularly inventive manner. Many of the textile and wallpaper patterns of the period are well worth reproducing and it is to be hoped that some will be available in the near future.

This book has been made possible by the Silver Studio Collection, at Middlesex University. This consists of the entire contents of the Silver Studio which were donated to the Middlesex University (formerly Hornsey College of Art) by Miss Mary Peerless in 1967. Miss Peerless is the step-daughter of Rex Silver, who had taken over the management of the studio in 1901. Probably no other collection of decorative design material so accurately or completely represents English small-house decoration. From

1, Preceding pages: Traditional floral patterns were always popular. This Silver Studio chintz is from 1924.

2, Right: A typical prosperous middle-class drawing-room circa 1890. ALthough there is no dado or frieze, strips of neo-Adam wallpaper are used to frame large panels of an elaborate Persian wallpaper. Note the fashionable use of numerous small tables to display large quantities of ornaments, flowers and photographs.

1880, when Arthur Silver opened the studio, until its close in 1963, many thousands of designs for wallpapers, textiles, carpets and linoleums were produced which eventually found their way into modest houses. The Silvers themselves lived in charming suburban houses and many of the shop catalogues illustrated in this book were used by the family for the purchase of their own household furniture and fittings.

Arthur Silver was born in Reading in 1853. His grandfather is recorded as having a cabinet-making business in Reading in 1837; his father, James Silver, described himself in the Reading Trade Directory of 1865 as an 'Upholster, Cabinetmaker, paper-hanger, estate agent, valuer, undertaker and agent to the Eagle Life Office'. In fact the diverse range of services offered was typical of the country town upholsterer in England in the mid-nineteenth century. Before the advent of department stores in the late nineteenth century, it was customary when setting up home to go to the local upholsterer, who would not only provide everything to go into the house, but would often undertake to procure the house as well. Increasing prosperity in late nineteenth-century England meant it was no longer necessary for one individual to fulfil so many roles in order to make a living; in the case of the Silver family, it became posible to specialize in cabinet-making and upholstery alone. From Arthur's point of view, however, a better childhood could not be imagined.

He was brought up surrounded by every conceivable type of furnishing fabric and wallpaper – from the heavy damasks and brocades used by the prosperous shopkeepers of Reading, to the Nottingham lace and cheap machine-printed wallpapers used in humble dwellings. The most popular of mid-Victorian textiles were hand woven and this early familiarity with them probably explains Arthur's great ability to design for these materials. An early interest in design can be assumed because in 1869 he attended Reading School of Art. This was one of the many schools of art established by Sir Henry Cole in an attempt to train a generation of designers who would satisfactorily unite art with industry. Although the impetus for design innovations in the late nineteenth century largely came from designers with an architectural background, there can be little doubt that these art schools did much to raise the level of visual awareness in England. Arthur did very well at Reading and some of his sketch-books from the period survive, full of enchanting botanical sketches and ornamental borders.

On leaving Reading in 1872, Arthur went to London where he was articled to one of the most fashionable designers of the day, HW Batley. Batley was very much in the vanguard of the Queen-Anne Revival, having previously achieved success in producing carpet designs in a ponderous Gothic style. By the 1870s that had been abandoned and he was producing designs for a very wide range of objects in an equally eclectic assortment of decorative styles. His furniture was largely in the Queen-Anne Revival style with broken pediments and classical ornamentation, but he was also one of the first English designers to use Japanese ornament. He was capable of

3 Design by HW Batley for a wallpaper or textile to complement the 'Louis' style of decorating, popular in the late nineteenth and early twentieth centuries.

working in the whole gamut of fashionable 1870s styles, from French Second Empire to Early Medieval. (This also reveals the vogue in the 1870s for historic styles, something which was then quite new.) Arthur could hardly have chosen a better master. His great ability to design for carpets was doubtless due to Batley, as was his ability to work in a vast range of styles – an essential requirement for a late Victorian designer. Perhaps most important of all were the contacts he was able to make. There was hardly a major manufacturer of wallpaper or textiles at that time who did not use Batley's designs. It would seem that Arthur established connections with these firms whilst still an apprentice and was also able to learn the technicalities involved. In later years he would often stress the necessity of a designer being able to understand the manufacturing process of the material for which he was designing.

4 Photograph of Arthur Silver and his wife Isabella Walenn. They were married in 1878 and this photograph was taken about 1885 by Fred Hollyer. Hollyer was a family friend who photographed just about everyone of artistic importance in late nineteenth-century London.

In 1878 Arthur married Isabella Walenn and they took the lease of a house at 132 Coningham Road, Shepherd's Bush, West London. Their first son Rex was born in 1879, and a year later, in 1880, Arthur took the decisive step of opening his own studio. He could not have chosen a better time to do so. As I shall explain in greater detail further on in this book, increasing prosperity in late nineteenth-century England had brought about a revolution in attitudes to home decoration. Prior to 1870 expressing much interest in interior decoration was thought to be rather vulgar. There were set conventions to be obeyed in decoration and furnishing. One chose an upholsterer according to one's means and was guided by him. Although in the 1860s and 70s *Punch* made fun of those aesthetes who tried to make their surroundings as artistic as possible, matters had settled down by the 1880s and the great devotion to home decoration that affected all but the poorest is one of the most endearing aspects of late Victorian domestic life.

Prices of household goods were falling rapidly in the late nineteenth century, and middle-class incomes rising. Combined with a growing interest in design, Arthur Silver's career could hardly fail to prosper. He stated in an interview in *The Studio* magazine in 1894:

> 'When I found, as every successful designer must needs discover sooner or later, that one pair of hands could not execute the orders which fell to my share, I attempted to bring together a body of men and establish a studio which would be capable of supplying designs for the whole field of fabrics and other materials used in the decoration of the house.'

In the early 1880s he continued Batley's practice of providing complete interior schemes, as well as designs for textiles and wallpapers. Two such schemes survive in the Silver Studio Collection (see illustration 7) but he found working for the general public fraught with difficulties. In a lecture on stencilling given to the Architectural Association in February, 1896 he remarked:

> '... the opportunities that I have had in the past for carrying out complete schemes of decoration, though not few, were so hampered by philistine prejudices that I turned my attention more exclusively than ever to designing and only availed myself of the rarer opportunities which occurred for unfettered treatments.'

This is hardly surprising, for one of the most exciting aspects of the 1880s and 90s was the way in which some manufacturers devoted themselves whole-heartedly to promoting good design. One of Arthur Silver's earliest and best customers was the firm of John Line. John Line was originally a furniture business in Reading, so it is very likely Arthur Silver knew the family well. When they established a wallpaper firm in London in 1892, Arthur designed all their publicity material, as well as being a major source of designs. His name was often mentioned in their advertisements, and other firms, notably Jeffrey & Co and Woollams, did this as well. It is apparent that as the market for good design in domestic furnishings grew, a tightly knit community of London-based designers and manufacturers evolved. The tightness of some of these interconnections can be further illustrated by the Silver-Aumonier friendship. Arthur's friend Frederic Aumonier was director of the firm William Woollams – one of the very best nineteenth-century wallpaper manufacturers, and which employed Arthur's designs with great frequency. A member of his family, Louisa Aumonier, worked as a designer

5 Design for a half-tester bed circa 1880, by Arthur Silver. Neo-Adam designs for furniture were very popular in the 1880s and 90s. The more elaborate French and English styles were particularly popular for bedrooms. Sadly, Arthur Silver designed almost no furniture after about 1885, concentrating almost wholly on textiles, wallpapers and floor-coverings.

for the Silver Studio in the 1890s, as did Stacy Aumonier, who later became well known as a light novelist and entertainer. The connections with manufacturers made by Arthur in the 1880s and 90s were to last throughout the history of the studio. Liberty's, Warners, GP & J Baker, Sanderson and John Line were still buying designs from Rex Silver in the 1960s.

Because of the support Arthur received in the early years of the studio, he found that business increased with great rapidity during the 1880s. The work he produced at this time was in a fashionably wide variety of styles. As we shall see, the late Victorian middle class had a passion for all sorts of historic ornament ranging from Jacobean to Second Empire and manufacturers required the Silver Studio to produce textile and wallpaper designs which would meet this demand. Thus we find Arthur Silver producing avant-garde Japanese-influenced wallpaper patterns and, at the same time, Empire silks for Princess May of Teck's wedding trousseau. During the 1880s and 90s much of the studio's bread-and-butter work was in producing designs which were strongly influenced by William Morris – in particular Morris's lush designs of the mid 1870s, such as *Myrtle* and *Acanthus*. Morris wallpapers, being hand-block printed, were extremely expensive, so a number of wallpaper manufacturers, anxious to profit from the popularity of these papers, asked Arthur Silver for similar designs which could be machine printed.

Like most good designers working in the late nineteenth century, Arthur Silver frequently used the collections of historic textiles at the Victoria and Albert Museum as a source of inspiration for his own designs. Because such extensive use was made of the V&A's collections, Arthur Silver, in 1889, decided to launch a series of large-scale photographs of what he considered to be the most significant of these textiles. He called his collection of photographs *The Silvern Series*. This enterprise attracted a considerable amount of publicity in the national press. His father ensured that his local paper mentioned his son's success. *The Berkshire Chronicle* of 24th August 1889, stated:

> '... a valuable work... has been suggested by Mr Arthur Silver, son of Mrs James Silver of this town... A new attempt to widen the usefulness of the splendid designs in South Kensington and other national collections has been conceived and carried out by Mr Arthur Silver, himself a well-known art designer.'

It is significant that the *Silvern Series* of photographs sold steadily throughout the 1890s, in particular to the more progressive firms such as Templeton's of Glasgow, whose carpets were famous for the quality of their designs. Other well-known purchasers were Warners, GP & J Baker and Liberty. The photographs themselves are of great use to us, for here we can see much of the original source material for Silver Studio designs of the 1880s and 90s. They fall into two distinct categories: small formalized patterns typified by

6, Right: Design for a wall decoration circa 1885 by Arthur Silver. Neo-Adam decoration was becoming increasingly popular in the 1880s and this scheme was probably intended for an expensive wallpaper by a firm such as Woollams.

7, Far right: Design for a door and wall decoration circa 1885, by Arthur Silver. Arthur Silver quite often designed complete interior schemes in the 1880s and this is a typical trial section. Here we can see clearly the fashionable division of the wall into three main sections of dado, filling and frieze. Note the influence of Japanese art in the design of the dado paper and the frieze.

8 Traditional carpet design, circa 1890, by
Arthur Silver. Naturalistic flowers and rococo
scroll-work were typical of carpet patterns at
this time.

9 Design for a printed textile circa 1890, by
Arthur Silver. This is a delightful and typically
aesthetic design, probably intended as a
Liberty's Art Furnishing textile.

Near Eastern silks; and (by far the greatest number) large, swirling patterns of acanthus scrolls and other classical motifs from sixteenth- and seventeenth-century European textiles and hangings, including Italian woven silks, English embroidery and Spanish embossed leather. Arthur Silver did not intend that these photographs should be copied exactly, rather he hoped that manufacturers would ask him to adapt them to produce designs which suited contemporary taste.

This and other schemes, such as his ambitious project to encourage a renewed use of stencilling in English houses, brought the work of Arthur Silver to the attention of a number of influential critics and designers. Walter Crane became a very good friend of his and encouraged Arthur to exhibit at the annual exhibitions of the Arts and Crafts Exhibition Society. He exhibited at most major exhibitions, including the *Paris Exposition Universelle Internationale* of 1889 and the World's Columbian Exposition at Chicago in 1893. His name was frequently linked with Walter Crane, William Morris, Lewis F Day and Christopher Dresser in contemporary newspaper articles. Perhaps most useful of all was his friendship with Gleeson White. Gleeson White was the first editor of the most influential and important journal devoted to the decorative arts in the late nineteenth century – *The Studio*.

Gleeson White devoted two lengthy articles to Arthur Silver in 1894 and 1895 and also asked him to contribute three sections (on designing for printed textiles, woven textiles and floorcloths) for his book *Practical Designing* (1894). Arthur could not have had a better ally. Almost everyone in England involved in the decorative arts read *The Studio* magazine, and it was also very widely read, and of great influence, in the United States and in Europe. The publicity Arthur received through this journal must have gone a long way to helping him build up business connections on both continents. (Indeed, by the early 1900s Rex Silver was selling more designs to France, Belgium and the United States than in Britain.)

Sadly, very little information about the designers Arthur Silver employed has survived. He doubtless kept detailed records of his staff but these were probably destroyed when his son Rex moved the studio from 84, Brook Green to 1, Haarlem Road. Certainly a number of important figures in British design history worked at the Studio or, like Christopher Dresser, sent relations there to gain practical experience. Indeed, so successful did the Silver Studio become in the 1890s that Henry Batley used his erstwhile apprentice as an agent to sell his designs – as did CFA Voysey in the 1920s. However, there can be little doubt that three particularly talented designers in the 1890s helped to establish the Silver Studio as England's largest source of designs in a style which we now call Art Nouveau. Two of them appear to have joined the studio in the early 1890s. These were Harry Napper and John Illingworth Kay. Both had highly distinctive styles. Illingworth Kay greatly admired Japanese prints and many of his designs were based on Oriental landscapes and often had a strong vertical emphasis. Napper's designs were

10 & 11 Two photographs of the Silver Studio, 1 Haarlem Road, Brook Green, Hammersmith. These pictures give a marvellous evocation of a traditional design studio where large collections of working designs were kept amidst all the ephemera thought necessary to provide visual inspiration. These photographs were taken in 1967 shortly before the contents of the Silver Studio were donated to Middlesex University by Rex Silver's step-daughter, Miss Mary Peerless. Rex Silver had bought this building in 1912 after selling the old studio house at No 3 Haarlem Road.

even more stylized and were frequently based on flattened oval flower forms, swirling upward growths and very sharply delineated outlines. Both designers suffered in some respects from working under the name of the Silver Studio, which in turn was rarely credited by the manufacturer. Nevertheless, works by both men were frequently illustrated in foreign periodicals and particularly in *Der Moderne Stil*. Such was the demand for avant-garde work that virtually the entire Silver Studio was given over to the production of Art Nouveau designs from 1895 to the early 1900s. The third designer was Archibald Knox, who became justly famous for his exquisite Art Nouveau designs for Liberty's Cymric and Tudric metalwork. His involvement with the Silver Studio is a matter of some speculation. The studio first started designing metalwork for Liberty in 1898. This was two years after the

12, Right: Wallpaper design, 1899.

*13 & 14, Far right:*Two photographs of Arthur Silver's house at 84 Brook Green, Hammersmith. These were probably taken in the mid-1890s. Arthur Silver had bought the house in 1884 and subsequently added a studio in the attic in 1896. They are marvellous examples of how an artistic middle-class house of the late nineteenth century was decorated. In these rooms one can see the growing fashion of combining genuine antique and reproduction furniture. Illustration 13 shows some of Arthur Silver's collection of Japanese prints. Much of the studio's work of the 80s and 90s was inspired by Japanese art. Illustration 14 is of the drawing-room chimney piece and shows *Days of Creation* gesso panel designed by Arthur Silver and executed by his assistant Harry Napper in 1892.

death of Arthur Silver, and whilst Harry Napper was manager of the studio. It was probable that Napper introduced Knox to the Silver Studio and that Knox collaborated with Rex Silver on the many designs that they produced for bowls, vases, buckles and clasps and candlesticks that were sold to Liberty from 1898 to the early 1900s.

Arthur Silver died in 1896 at the age of forty-three. He had achieved a very great deal in the sixteen years since he opened the Silver Studio. He had bought an attractive Queen-Anne Revival house, No 84 Brook Green, in 1884, added a studio to it in 1886 and in 1893 had bought No 3 Haarlem Road, directly behind 84 Brook Green, also to use as a studio. In order to do this he had been forced to borrow money from his father, friends and from a building society. With a family to provide for as well, he had of necessity to

15 Photograph of Rex Silver, Arthur Silver's eldest son, taken about 1910. Rex ran the Silver Studio from 1901 until it closed in 1963.

16 Photograph of Harry Silver, taken about 1910. Harry Silver ran the Silver Studio in partnership with his brother Rex from 1901 until 1916 when he left to join the army.

17, Right: The rather deep colours and tapestry feel of this design were very popular circa 1915.

work extremely hard. However, there can be no doubt that he ranks as one of the greatest of late nineteenth century designers. His European reputation as an avant-garde English designer was continued by Harry Napper, who took over the management of the Silver Studio in December, 1896.

Harry Napper ran the Silver Studio with great flair until 1898 when, as Arthur had done after HW Batley, he decided to set up a practice of his own. Another studio designer, JR Houghton, continued to manage the studio until 1901, when Arthur's two sons, Rex and Harry, were old enough to assume full control. Both Napper and Houghton had continued Arthur's successful sale of designs to American and European manufacturers. Some of the best known included Bergerot, Dupont et Cie, Dumas, Florquin, Gros Roman, Zuher, Vanoutryve, Parison and Leborgne. The most important American customers at this time were Macy and Marshall Field, but it was not until the 1920s that the American market became very important for the studio.

Continental manufacturers used English Art Nouveau textile designs as a basis for developing new directions in pattern design. The English middle class, as we shall see, regarded Art Nouveau as a quaint modern style, an

18 The drawing-room of a substantial house photographed in 1902. Up-to-date Art Nouveau wallpapers, textiles and light paintwork are combined with classical mouldings and Victorian knick-knacks.

19, *Right:* Design for a printed textile in the fashionably deep colours of 1895.

alternative to Louis XVI or Queen-Anne, and by 1910 it was thoroughly out of date, suitable only for cheap wallpapers. A new middle-class decorating style had been gradually evolving since the 1890s. It was a style that evoked the charms of pre-Industrial Revolution country houses, and which was characterized by chintz patterns and antique or reproduction antique furniture. Leaders of taste since the mid-nineteenth century had been demanding a simple and unpretentious attitude to interior decoration – simple rooms containing well-designed and constructed furniture accompanied by functional and beautiful objects. By the early 1890s, a number of architects and designers were advocating a simple approach to decoration, and following William Morris they frequently referred to unspoilt small country house interiors as a decidedly more satisfactory alternative to the over-elaborate and dark urban middle-class home. Architects like William Lethaby were anxious that the working classes should also copy simple country-house interiors, suggesting that plain whitewash and solid oak

furniture were infinitely preferable to cheap gaudy wallpapers and second-hand veneered rosewood.

Just as Arthur Silver had done, Rex and Harry saw the necessity of being able to produce designs in a wide variety of styles. As the vogue for Art Nouveau declined in the early 1900s, they concentrated increasingly on the production of designs in historic styles. Rex dealt with the administration of the studio, while his brother Harry acted as design manager. The Silver Studio's entry for *The Studio Year Book Directory of Designers* of 1909 was as follows:

> 'Messrs R and H Silver are young designers who work together at their Studios at No 3 Haarlem Road, Brook Green, W, with two or three young assistants to aid them in carrying out their ideas. They lay themselves out to supply designs in the different styles both ancient and modern and owing to their knowledge of the different branches of weaving and printing etc, all their designs for such purposes as Wallpapers, Cretonnes, Tapestries, etc are thoroughly practical. They are also able to design and carry out schemes for interior decoration and are able to use for this purpose certain new stencilling processes which enable them to obtain very individual and complete effects for walls and all kinds of hangings – combining the two to make complete decorations to rooms etc.'

Particularly popular with middle-class home decorators in the early years of the twentieth century were chinoiserie chintz patterns – flowering branches, tropical birds, cabbage roses and pagodas. The Silver Studio produced thousands of such designs both for printed furnishing textiles and wallpapers.

Although the energy of the Arts and Crafts movement was very much on the wane by the outbreak of the First World War, Rex and Harry were doing very well at the Silver Studio. Commissions from the USA and France were still pouring in, and English manufacturers were buying their designs with great enthusiasm. In 1914 the Silvers had eleven designers and four apprentices. Although the Silver Studio eventually had to close until 1918, this was due solely to the staff, including Rex and Harry, being conscripted. However, by 1920 the Silver Studio was back to its pre-war strength, with two highly efficient secretaries, Miss Cook and Miss Varney, maintaining accurate records of the Silver Studio's commissions. Harry Silver did not return to the studio after the war but his place as design manager was filled by Herbert Crofts who worked at the studio until his death in 1937. As we shall see further on in this book, small-house decoration was divided into two distinct categories during the inter-war period. For the majority, the war had, if anything, given added impetus to the desire to make one's house look as antique as possible. Dark varnished paintwork, old oak or mahogany furniture and endless reproduction chintz-patterned printed textiles. The upper middle classes bought genuine antique furniture and hand block-

20 Early twentieth-century drawing-room paper.

21 After the First World War, bright strong colours, usually combined with black, became popular. This 'Ideal Home' interior shows how exotic motifs could be introduced – the Chinese pelmet and lampshades contrast quite happily with Heppelwhite chairs and eighteenth-century wall panels.

22 Working-class kitchen, 1935. Although many less well-off people had to use Victorian furniture in the 1930s, at least it was possible to afford new wallpaper. Here we see a modernist paper and accompanying narrow frieze in use.

printed copies of early Victorian chintzes. The lower middle classes bought poorly made reproduction furniture and machine-printed cotton, but both were striving after the same effect. For a minority, however, the war had inspired a desire for brilliant colouring and exotic designs; the Silver Studio catered for this on two levels – it was able to provide simple abstract patterns inspired by the best of French design of the 1920s, and at the same time created some wonderfully opulent chinoiserie wallpapers in rich lacquer colour schemes such as red, black and gold.

By the outbreak of the Second World War the output of the Silver Studio was larger and more varied than at any other time in its history. The whole gamut of modest English home decorating was reflected in its work – neo-Regency, neo-Gothic, simple early nineteenth-century chintzes and seventeenth-century needlework designs. The studio did simple textured patterns for woven textiles and single-leaf motifs for both woven and printed textiles. Cubist wallpapers and textiles were very popular until the mid 1950s, particularly lower down the social scale.

Rex Silver managed to keep the studio going throughout the war, although most of his staff, including his two secretaries, left. Two of his best designers, however, remained. They were Frank Price and Lewis Jones. One of his outside designers, HC Bareham continued to work for Rex up until the studio closed down in 1963. The Festival of Britain and Scandinavian modernism rather passed the Silver Studio by. Throughout the war and up until the 1960s, the Silver Studio specialized in providing neo-eighteenth century and Regency designs, largely for the studio's oldest customers – R Denby & Sons, Liberty, Sanderson, Simpson & Godlee, Turnbull & Stockdale, Warner and GP & J Baker. Rex was used to dealing with these firms who in turn could rely on the Silver Studio to produce period patterns of superb quality. It was during the period 1940 to 1963 that the studio's work failed to be completely representative of ordinary taste. From the period 1880 up until 1940 there can be no other collection in the world which so accurately reflects the types of wallpapers and textiles which went into the English middle-class house. We shall now proceed to examine the interiors of these houses in detail.

23 Modernist rug design, 1934 by John Churton of the Silver Studio. Designs such as these were very popular for less expensive textiles and wallpapers.

24 Brilliantly coloured 1920s 'futurist' textile.

PART·ONE: 1880-1895

VICTORIAN·DEVOTION To·THE·DELIGHTS·OF HoME·DECORATION

By any standards, the prosperous middle-class house of circa 1890 was decorated with an awe-inspiring richness. The walls were papered in colours so dark and varnished that entering the hall of an ordinary suburban villa must have resembled stepping into an old oil painting that had never been cleaned. Who nowadays would use three different kinds of densely patterned wallpaper on one wall, each separated by an elaborately moulded rail, or use four different kinds of plain and patterned velvet on one armchair? Yet this was common practice in the 1880s and 1890s. Indeed, examples of such interiors survived well into the 1950s in obscure seaside boarding houses and private hotels in spa towns. Nottingham lace hung at every window, monstrously healthy aspidistras planted in treacle-glazed 'art' pots flourished in dark Minton-tiled halls, Japanese screens, lavishly decorated with storks, gave protection from draughts in sitting-rooms and everywhere endless small tables were carefully piled with books, framed photographs, small pieces of porcelain and pots of ferns. It was all elaborately intended to impress the visitor with the owner's appreciation of the decorative arts and evinced the desire for a truly artistic home. These interiors we have now come to think of as typically Victorian, yet only a few years before 1880, the middle-class house was done up in a very different way.

The every-day mid-Victorian interior is described in the most disparaging of detail in many of the books on home decoration which were published in the late nineteenth century. Probably the most popular (and certainly by far the most readable) of these were written by Mrs JE Panton, the daughter of the famous nineteenth-century artist WP Frith. Intelligent and well connected, she had married a country brewer. She turned to writing on interior decoration both as a palliative to boredom and from the necessity to earn money. Her first book on her experiences of decorating her own houses both in the country and in London suburbia was *From Kitchen to Garrett* published in 1889. It was an enormous success and ran into many editions. The few earlier books on home decoration such as Eastlake's *Hints on Household Taste* were aimed at the upper end of the middle class. In any case, they tended to lack real practical information. Mrs Panton named specific colours and patterns for wallpapers and textiles and the shops where these could be bought. Her ideas were affordable by those on a respectable middle-class income of £350 to £750 per annum and were presented in an almost irresistibly forceful manner. Not only did her decorative schemes accurately reflect late Victorian middle-class taste, but her remarks about the problems of setting up home in the 1860s and 70s are an invaluable clue to how the previous generation decorated their houses. Her descriptions of mid-Victorian tastes and interiors serve to emphasize the revolution in approach to home decoration that made 1880 such a fortuitous year for Arthur Silver to open his own studio of design.

A suburban villa in congenial surroundings had always been a Victorian

1, Preceding pages: Design for a wallpaper circa 1885 by Arthur Silver. This is an old-fashioned chintz paper which would have been used for bedrooms.

2 Contemporary photograph of a middle-class drawing-room of the 1890s. Here we can see the large quantity of different furnishing textiles that were so popular in the 1890s. Muslin and lace are used on chair backs and for curtains.

3 Detail from *Past and Present* by Augustus Egg showing the interior of a typical mid-Victorian drawing-room.

middle-class ambition. Indeed one has only to read contemporary descriptions of life in nineteenth-century London to see why, by 1880, only the very rich and very poor remained in the West End. The problem was largely one of too many people trying to live and work in towns which were not built or planned to cope with such numbers. As England's wealth continued to grow, so more and more people earned a salary which enabled them to achieve a middle class way of life. As a consequence the suburban expansion of London and other cities grew apace. During the 1850s, 60s and 70s a number of manuals on housekeeping were published to instruct those new to the ranks of the middle-class on the correct way to run their houses. Mrs Beeton's *Household Management* is the most famous of these but there were others which are now of more use to us, such as Cassell's *Household Guide* and Walsh's *Manual of Domestic Economy*. Both offer advice for those on lower salaries than Mrs Beeton's readership and both provide far more useful clues to attitudes to home decoration in the mid-nineteenth century. Whilst information is rarely volunteered on the aesthetics of home decoration, very specific information is given on the contents of the respectable home. Walsh actually lists the contents one would expect to find in every room of the middle-class house. Cassell's *Household Guide* suggests appropriate papers and textiles for each room as well as offering a multitude of ideas for the embellishment and decoration of the house. While the quality of the contents might vary according to income, it is apparent that the interiors of middle-class houses were remarkably unified. There is even a consistency about the decorative treatment of the exterior – Walsh recommends oak graining and varnishing as the standard decoration for all external woodwork. Interior woodwork was also grained and varnished but a wide variety of timber could be imitated, including mahogany, oak, walnut and satinwood. (These were all popular for furniture at this time.) Most late nineteenth-century writers on interior decoration shared Ruskin's detestation of graining, although Mrs Panton thought it acceptable for the back staircase. Despite this, graining continued to be the most common treatment of internal woodwork until the late 1930s.

A brief description of the decoration of the mid-Victorian small house is not out of place here as it will serve to emphasize the remarkable transformation that occurred after 1880, when to take an interest in home decoration became an almost universal fashion.

The most common treatment for the hall was to hang an imitation marble paper on the walls and to grain the woodwork a dark colour. The floor covering was almost invariably a narrow strip of dark brown or green oil cloth (often with a white and yellow Greek key pattern to the edges) with the floor surrounds grained to match the wainscot. The only furniture in the hall would be a mahogany hat stand or hall table with a marble top and one or two upright chairs, if space permitted. In more prosperous homes the hall might form the repository for a romantic interest in natural history and be used to display cases of stuffed birds and animals.

Very strict conventions were attached to the equipping of both drawing- and dining-rooms. Cassell's *Household Guide* recommended an imitation watered silk paper for drawing-rooms, perhaps ornamented with bunches of gilt flowers tied with ribbons. Eighteenth-century French decoration was becoming increasingly popular at this time. For the drawing-room, at least one sofa was obligatory as were two armchairs and a selection of upright chairs. These were upholstered in horsehair and given protective covers of glazed chintz. Other standard equipment for the drawing-room was a large gilt pier-glass for above the chimney piece and a large circular or loo table at which one could read or work. It was customary for there to be a small

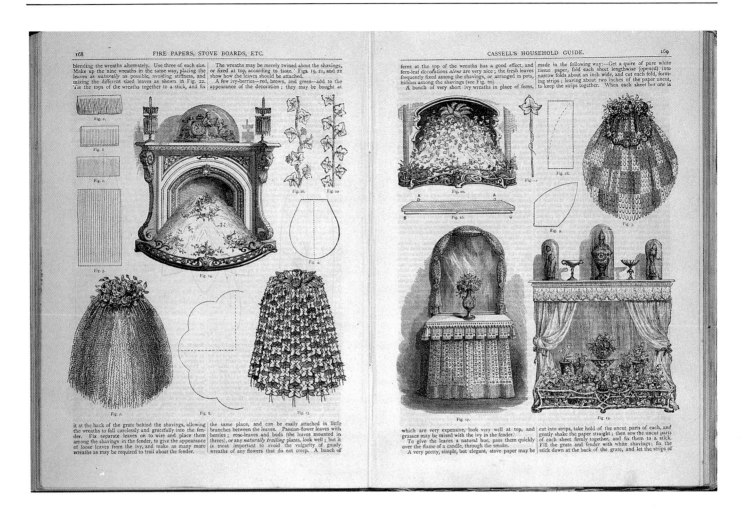

4 Illustrations of decorations for fireplaces from Cassell's *Household Guide* circa 1870. Decorations for empty hearths were very popular in the mid-nineteenth century and ranged from pot plants and bark to elaborate mounds of shredded muslin decorated with dried or paper flowers.

marble-topped chiffonier or sideboard and perhaps card and sewing tables. A fitted carpet was always recommended for the drawing-room, either an Axminster or velvet pile, and an elaborate pattern such as cabbage roses and acanthus scrolls was thought perfectly desirable. Ornaments tended to reflect an intense interest in natural history – glass cases of ferns, elaborate freshwater or marine aquariums, cabinets of fossils and shells. In the summer, heavy curtains of damask or moreen were taken down to be substituted by white muslin. (Its colour was improved by exposure to sunlight.) The empty hearth was filled with bark-fronted boxes containing ferns, ivy and geraniums; alternatively a mountain of shredded muslin would be decorated with dried or artificial flowers.

For the dining-room, dark red silk flock wallpaper was considered the height of perfection. It rapidly became encrusted with grime and was impossible to clean, but it imparted a richness to the room that could be achieved in no other way. It also made the ideal foil for gilt-framed paintings

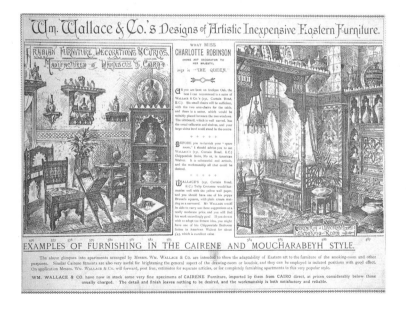

5 Drawing-room designed by HW Batley for the cabinet-makers Collinson & Lock, illustrated in *Decoration* magazine, October, 1884. Arthur Silver had been apprenticed to HW Batley who had taught him to design complete interiors. Here Batley has produced a Queen-Anne Revival style drawing-room. Note the elaborate overmantel and panelled dado.

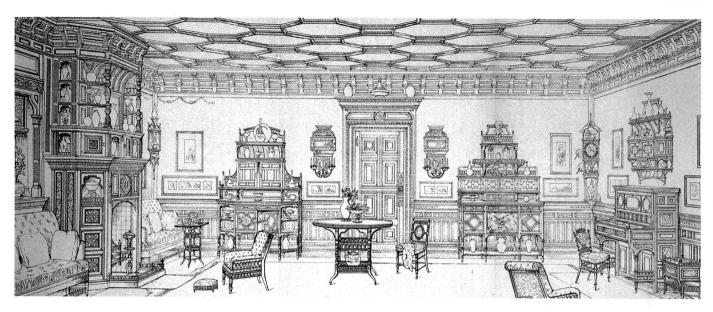

6 Catalogue illustration of Arabian furniture, circa 1895. Exotic furniture, in this instance Arabian, was very popular in more prosperous middle-class households. It was felt to be particularly suited to smoking and billiard rooms, conjuring up the pleasures of the harem.

7 & 8, *Above and right:* Two designs of the early 1880s for expensive wallpapers by Arthur Silver. Here we can see the popular late eighteenth-century practice of ransacking the more elaborate historical styles to produce patterned wallpapers for the dado, filling and frieze.

which explains why it was such a popular choice for public art galleries. Massive mahogany furniture was universally recommended for this room and was the bane of all writers on home decoration in the 1880s and 90s. Mrs Panton wrote:[1]

> 'Do you recollect . . . the orthodox dining-room of twenty-five years ago? – the heavy, thick curtains of red or green cloth or moreen damask; the tremendous mahogany sideboard, generally with a cellarette underneath it, which, I recollect, made an admirable tomb in which to bury one's dolls or obnoxious books . . .'

Like the drawing-room, one was encouraged to have a fitted carpet, but in a real or fake Turkey pattern of reds, blues and greens.

Perhaps one of the greatest differences in home decoration between the mid and late nineteenth century lay in attitudes to the furnishing and decoration of the bedroom. In the 1850s and 60s the purchase of beds and their appropriate bed-hangings was probably the biggest single outlay the householder made. Great care was taken in the choice of mattress, be it a wool 'French' one, a more traditional feather bed, or hair. Flock was considered suitable only for servants. Prices varied enormously according to quality but it was universally agreed that this was not an area to economize. Vast sums were also spent on bed drapery. Four-poster beds, although considered old fashioned by 1860, were still seen as status symbols and upholsterers were anxious to encourage this particularly lucrative aspect of their work. Damask was still the preferred choice for bed-hangings, lined with a coloured and glazed calico. Chintz or dimity was sometimes advocated for summer use. It was also customary to drape dressing tables in pink calico, covered with white lace. The other usual furniture for bedrooms included chests of drawers, wardrobes and washing stands. Mahogany was the most usual wood, but in more prosperous households walnut and satinwood were to be found. The problem of bed bugs in large cities discouraged the use of wallpaper as it provided a refuge for insects. For similar reasons fitted carpets were never recommended for bedrooms, indeed bare boards which could easily be washed were perfectly admissible.

Although growing prosperity and increasing artistic awareness were important catalysts in the late nineteenth-century decorating revolution, fashionable reaction to the previous generation's taste must be cited as a crucial factor. Mrs Panton recalled that, because everything cost so much in the 1860s, goods were bought primarily for durability. She wrote in 1919:[2]

> 'Fifty years ago, if carpets and curtains were bought at all, it was after high and long debates in the family and heavens how they wore!'

She also wrote at length of the lack of interest in decoration in the mid-nineteenth century and how surplus money was usually spent on expensive food and drink, rather than on the home, or books or travel. By 1890 the possession of an artistically decorated house was an almost universal middle-class ambition. It was during this period that home decoration became increasingly seen as a purely feminine occupation. Most writers on the subject were middle-class women and the magazines that most often featured articles on decoration were intended for a largely female readership. *Queen* and *The Lady's Pictorial* were two of the most popular. By 1890 the middle-class woman had both more money to spend and more leisure time in which to spend it than her mid-Victorian counterpart. Increased prosperity was reflected in more domestic help, and it was becoming more usual for the middle-class woman to hand over the running of the house to servants, whilst dealing solely with the administrative aspects of housekeeping. Home decoration was one of the few acceptable outlets she had for artistic and creative talents. Increasingly, shops encouraged the middle-class woman to exercise those talents to the full. During the 1870s and 80s, many of the big Tottenham Court Road furniture stores such as Maples, Shoolbred, Heals and Oetzmann, began the now ubiquitous practice of displaying their goods in the form of room settings. Their catalogues, which were sent to provincial customers, contained lavish illustrations of room sets, with texts by well-known writers on decoration such as Mrs Panton and Colonel Edis. This must have encouraged and disseminated new ideas in furnishings and room layouts to a degree that had hitherto been impossible. Such was the popularity of this method of displaying household goods that many magazines carried reviews of them. Previously most people bought their furniture, textiles and wallpaper from their local upholsterer. Arthur Silver's father was a typical country upholsterer, supplying everything to do with the house from drawing-room sofas to arranging fire insurance. Unless the upholsterer was particularly expensive and famous, the range of patterns and styles on offer tended to be extremely limited. By 1890 the middle-class housewife could spend a day in London looking at a bewildering array of furniture, textiles and wallpapers presented in a way which would help her to visualize them in use in her own house.

However, a great cause of confusion at this time was the custom on the part of both manufacturers and retailers to attribute a specific historic style to their goods. Armchairs that bore no resemblance to eighteenth-century French furniture were glibly labelled Louis XVI and massive and be-mirrored sideboards with storks carved on the panels of the doors were sold as Anglo-Japanese. The ordinary public usually had no idea what a Louis XVI chair looked like and were obliged to follow the advice of the salesman or the recommendations of writers in magazines. It is small wonder that the demand for practical furnishing guides grew so quickly at this time. The wholesale ransacking of an increasingly wide range of historic styles of ornament had been going on since the 1860s. Most designers made much use of the Victoria and Albert Museum as a source of inspiration and Arthur

Silver was no exception to this. He had been taught by HW Batley to produce faithful copies of historic English and European ornament. He had also been introduced to Japanese art, which by 1880 was a national craze. The 'Queen-Anne' style was equally popular and was to have a lasting influence on middle-class decorating taste. As a decorating style it was given a very loose interpretation indeed. Any piece of furniture that had turned supports and a classical pediment was liable to be given this appellation. But significantly, it was to lead to the desire to give one's home an antique and quaint appearance and the earliest manifestations of this were in the reappearance of picturesque internal fitments such as dados and built-in cupboards. It was also to lead to the fashion for collecting real antique furniture that has been such a feature of twentieth-century middle-class taste.

The contrast between the fashionably decorated suburban house of 1860 and a similar property in 1890 was very great indeed. What one must remember is that changes were gradual and many people were obliged either through poverty or lack of inclination to retain their gilt pier-glasses and marble chiffoniers but as a writer in *The Builder* remarked:[3]

'. . . this indifference to the aesthetics of house furniture and decoration can hardly be openly professed by any who have the hope of social salvation.'

The changes that had taken place were instantly evident on entering the hall of the 1890s villa. It had become an almost universal fashion to divide the hall into three distinct horizontal sections – the dado from the skirting to about 3ft 6in from the floor, the filling from dado rail to picture rail and finally the frieze from picture rail to ceiling cornice. This provided scope for a wide variety of interesting treatments and designers and wallpaper manufacturers gave much thought to creating rich and opulent papers for each section. Dense and organic designs based on stylized flowers and foliage were by far the most popular wallpaper patterns in the 1880s and 90s. (It should be remembered that this was a time when plainness and simplicity were equated with poverty and so to be avoided at all costs.) By 1890 William Morris was a household name but few could afford his block-printed wallpapers and chintzes. Manufacturers of machine-printed textiles and wallpapers bought designs from Arthur Silver which had a close resemblance to Morris's more elaborate designs. These could subsequently be sold to the public at a fraction of the cost of Morris's originals. With their vigorous acanthus scroll-work patterns in gloomy secondary and tertiary colours, these were felt to be ideal for narrow suburban halls. The dado was to survive in halls and dining-rooms until the end of the 1930s. It was nearly always dark, as it served a practical as well as decorative function, protecting walls in areas of particularly heavy wear. Many writers in the 1890s recommended imitation Cordoba leather dados for their durability and resistance to grime; Lincrusta and the much cheaper anaglypta were also very

9 Design for a wallpaper circa 1880 by Arthur Silver. Reproductions of elaborate eighteenth-century styles such as this were still in great demand for traditional drawing-room wallpapers in the 1880s and early 90s.

10 Design for a printed furnishing textile circa 1895 probably by Arthur Silver. This is typical of the reproductions of William Morris patterns that the studio executed in the 80s and 90s.

11 Contemporary photograph of a hall. Although the picture was probably taken in the 1890s, the hall has been decorated in a typically mid-nineteenth century manner. There is a linoleum printed to imitate Minton tiles, stuffed birds, sporting prints and oak-grained woodwork.

12 Right: Sheet of designs for encaustic tiling by Maw & Co, circa 1890. Tiles such as these were extensively used for halls, kitchens and bathrooms in late nineteenth-century houses.

popular choices. Indeed, many of the best designers of the late nineteenth century produced patterns for anaglypta, including Walter Crane and Christopher Dresser. Anaglypta had the advantage that it could be brush-grained to imitate wood and varnished for extra protection. By far the most popular wallpapers for the filling section of the hall, were 'sanitary' papers. These were papers which were printed with engraved copper rollers. This produced a very fine smooth surface which was then varnished, and so rendered washable – hence the term sanitary. Anyone who has ever stripped wallpaper off the hall of a house built before 1910 must surely have encountered such papers. As mentioned earlier, the colour and pattern quickly disappeared as the varnish darkened with exposure to atmospheric grime, resulting in a universal rich treacly brown. Arthur Silver designed hundreds of such papers. The designs which were most popular were those based on flowers such as the peony and chrysanthemum which lent themselves to a lush and organic interpretation. For the same reason acanthus leaf patterns and French eighteenth-century scroll-work were much favoured. It was usual to base the frieze pattern on that of the filling with one feature predominating, such as the leaf scroll. The hall floor in better class houses was generally tiled with encaustic tiles from a firm such as Minton. Pseudo-medieval patterns, severely geometric, were the most popular. For those without tiled floors, Arthur Silver designed linoleums which imitated encaustic tiling with considerable accuracy.

One of the most remarkable changes between 1860 and 1890 was the vast increase in the amount of textiles used in the ordinary home, and this was immediately noticeable in the hall. A great variety of richly coloured and patterned velvets, damasks, serges and machine-woven tapestries was now within the price range of the middle classes. Furnishing stores and upholsterers had a vested interest in encouraging their use, so elaborate portière curtains were recommended for every door. Trade and women's magazines frequently published patterns for these curtains and their accompanying pelmets and praised the sumptuous effect they lent to narrow halls and landings.

Great changes had taken place in the drawing-room too. The old formal layout of centre table, upright chairs, chiffonier and sofa was fast disappearing and instead a much more informal approach was being adopted with the emphasis on comfort, prettiness and interesting colour schemes. It was quite usual in the 1880s and 90s to have a dado in the drawing-room, sometimes of a textile such as chintz or cretonne, or perhaps a Japanese grass paper. Above would be the main filling wallpaper – always in secondary and tertiary colours and instantly making the room dark. Similar patterns to those used in the hall were popular – copies of Morris's more lush and organic papers of the 1870s, for instance. However, the walls were usually so densely hung with gilt-framed pictures and photographs that barely any wallpaper was visible. A particularly common device in the 80s

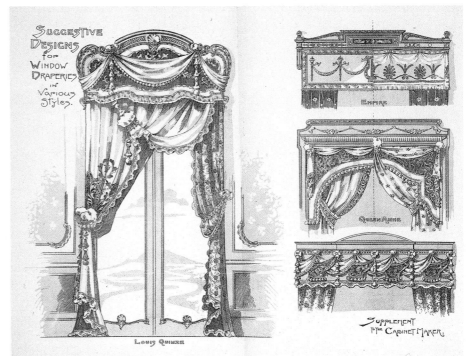

13 Illustration of examples of window drapery from *The Cabinet Maker & Art Furnisher* 1893-4. Here we can see not only the opulent use of furnishing textiles common at this time, but also the ubiquitous habit of crediting objects with quite erroneous historic styles.

and 90s was to divide the drawing-room by the use of fretwork arches, screens and shelves to create 'cosy corners'. These served to increase the informality of the room's layout – Mrs Panton recommended at least two, one for winter by the fireside and one for summer by the largest window. The centre table of the 1860s was replaced by numerous small tables, artfully positioned by the sides of armchairs and sofas. These were used to display an interesting accumulation of books, ornaments, lamps, photographs and sewing boxes, all testifying to their possessor's artistic and home-making interests. Gone, too, was the gilt pier-glass, to be replaced by the many-shelved and be-mirrored overmantel. This became an almost universal feature of the middle-class drawing-room; frequently in a Queen-Anne Revival style, and of mahogany, it was capable of displaying an imposing quantity of ornaments. The quantity of textiles in use in the middle-class drawing-room was very great. It was customary to upholster armchairs in at least two different woven textiles and with elaborate fringing. Loose covers continued to be very popular as they afforded protection from the ravages of dust from incessant coal fires. Like their mid-nineteenth-century counter-parts these were made from glazed chintz with a traditional pattern of naturalistic flowers in bright colours. The chimney piece would normally have an elaborately swagged valance and curtains which could be drawn to hide the empty hearth in summer. At the windows heavily patterned Nottingham lace curtains were usually hung, though Madras muslin was

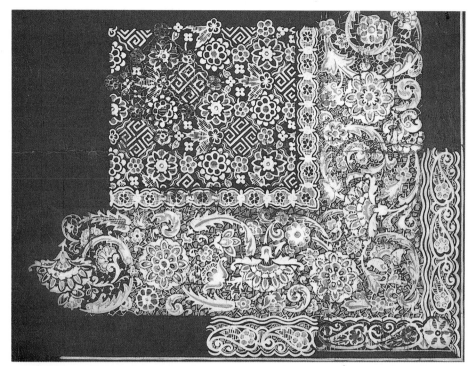

14 Design for a lace curtain, circa 1890, by Arthur Silver. Cotton lace curtains were used in virtually every house in the late nineteenth century, from cottage to mansion. Most were machine woven in Nottingham in a wide variety of patterns. Arthur Silver made a speciality of designing for them.

preferred by the more design-conscious: this was ordinary muslin which had a pattern woven into it. It was much softer in effect than Nottingham lace, and many important designers in the 1890s produced patterns for it. For the heavy curtains there was an almost unlimited choice of tapestries, velvets and brocades. A particularly important feature of the late nineteenth-century drawing-room was the amount of draping of objects that was carried out. Pianos, small tables, footstools – all could be covered in lace or plush. Even picture frames and plant pots could sport a silk or velvet bow. Equally evident was the intense admiration for Japanese art. The more prosperous and aesthetic bought Japanese prints and blue and white porcelain. In the ordinary suburban house people used Japanese silk scarves to tie back curtains and nailed Japanese fans to the dado rail. Importantly, this interest in Japanese art by designers led to the development of British Art Nouveau, as we shall see in the next section.

During the 1880s and 90s fitted carpets almost totally disappeared. This was largely due to an ever-increasing awareness of hygiene. Parquet flooring was the most favoured if it could be afforded and a wide choice of elaborate patterns was available. Failing this, the usual treatment was to stain the floorboards and then varnish and polish them. Many of the big West End stores carried a good stock of Turkish and Persian tribal carpets. William Morris's own carpets were also much sought after, though most people made do with Brussels and Axminster carpet squares and rugs.

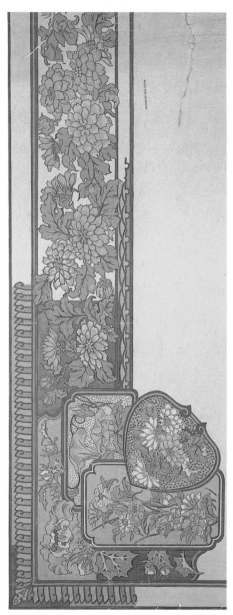

If the ideal drawing-room dripped femininity, a more masculine treatment was preferred for the dining-room. The more austere historic styles were favoured, such as François Premier or English Renaissance. There was also a growing tendency in the 1890s to use oak instead of the traditional mahogany. A dado was inevitable in this room, usually stained and varnished anaglypta but reproduction Spanish leather was particularly sought after. It was still surprisingly usual to cling to crimson as the colour for the filling paper, though reproduction tapestry papers in blues, browns and greens were thought more artistic. Although the walls could be densely hung with pictures and an elaborate overmantel was the rule, the necessity of serving food made too much clutter impractical. It was becoming increasingly popular in the middle-class homes to serve food from the sideboard, the maid handing dishes to the guests. The previous custom in England had been for the food to be placed on the table and for guests to help themselves. This change in method required that the layout of the dining-room be kept as simple as possible. However, it did mean that the table could be very elaborately decorated. Because the table was now no longer cluttered with tureens and dishes, quite wonderful arrangements of flowers and fruit were possible.

Like the rest of the house, bedrooms underwent dramatic changes. The heavily draped four-poster bed was universally condemned on both hygienic and artistic grounds; wooden bedsteads, however, were slowly returning to favour in the 1890s, despite the popularity of brass. (Wood was felt to be

15, Above: Design for a carpet border by Arthur Silver, circa 1885. This clearly shows the influence of Japanese art on popular textile design at this time.

16 Design for a dado paper, 1885, by Arthur Silver. A fashionable aesthetic movement design featuring Oriental motifs and peacock feathers. The particular shade of blue employed in this design was very popular in the 80s and 90s.

more appropriate for decorating in a historic style.) The desire for comfort and increased informality led many writers on decoration to encourage their readers to furnish their bedrooms as a species of boudoir, with sofas, armchairs, bookshelves and small desks. The elaborate eighteenth-century English and French styles with their opportunities for inlay and marquetry work were felt to be particularly appropriate. Mrs Panton wrote in 1896:[4]

> '... if she can visit Hewetson and have real old Chippendale toilet-tables, washing stands and wardrobes, she should certainly do so; if not, she should buy new things made on similar lines and these she can always find at Smee & Cobay's ...'

It is doubtful whether the English middle-class house has ever been so cluttered, or as opulently decorated and furnished as it was in the 1890s. Certainly one could not recreate this style in the 1980s unless one had a great deal of money. Nor would the sequestered gloom of these interiors be to everyone's taste. In the next section of this book we shall see how the influence of Art Nouveau and the Arts and Crafts movement led to a diminution of the clutter and a gradual use of lighter, clearer colours.

NOTES
1 Mrs JE Panton: *From Kitchen to Garrett*, 1889, pp 7-8.
2 Mrs JE Panton: *In Garrett & Kitchen*, 1919, p 18.
3 *The Builder*, 6th October 1877, p 1002.
4 Mrs JE Panton: *Suburban Residences & How to Circumvent Them*, 1896, p 244.

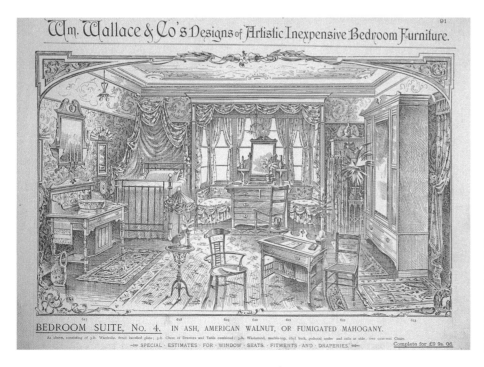

Wm. Wallace & Co's Designs of Artistic Inexpensive Bedroom Furniture.

BEDROOM SUITE, No. 4. IN ASH, AMERICAN WALNUT, OR FUMIGATED MAHOGANY.

As above, consisting of 3-ft. Wardrobe, fitted bevelled plate; 3-ft. Chest of Drawers and Table combined; 3-ft. Washstand, marble-top, tiled back, pedestal under and rails at side; two cane-seat Chairs.

SPECIAL · ESTIMATES · FOR · WINDOW · SEATS, FITMENTS · AND · DRAPERIES.

Complete for £9 9s. 0d.

17 Catalogue illustration of bedroom furniture, circa 1895. In this catalogue illustration we see how furniture was being shown in complete room settings. Customers were encouraged to buy entire suites of furniture, in this case in an artistic Queen-Anne Revival style. As in the contemporary photograph of a bedroom (illustration 21) much use is made of elaborately draped textiles.

18, Above left: Design for a carpet border by Harry Napper of the Silver Studio, 1894. Early Silver Studio Art Nouveau production of globe flowers and acanthus leaves in fashionable pale greens and terracotta.

19, Above right: Design for an Axminster carpet (filling and border) circa 1885 by Arthur Silver. Stylized flower and leaf pattern inspired by Persian art. This is a typical 'artistic' carpet design of the period in delicate tertiary colours.

20, Right: Carpet design, 1891, by Arthur Silver. Carpet patterns in the 80s and 90s tended to be traditional. This shows the continuing popularity of mid-nineteenth century French decorative design.

21, Above: Contemporary photograph of a middle-class bedroom circa 1895. Here we can see a masterpiece of the upholsterer's art. The pier-glass and chimney piece have been lavishly draped and the half-tester bed had been hung with brocade and Nottingham lace.

22 Design for a wallpaper, 1891, by Arthur Silver. This is a pretty Japanese-influenced design for use in artistic bedrooms and was probably intended for sale through Liberty's.

Nº 939.

23 Design for a bedroom wash-stand by Arthur Silver, circa 1880. This is in a delicate neo-Sheraton style, which had become popular in the 1870s.

24, Left: Design for a wallpaper, circa 1885 by Arthur Silver. A typical 'artistic' wallpaper of the 80s of a type most suited to bedrooms. The particular shade of greyish-blue used for the background was very fashionable at this time.

25, Far left: Design for a furnishing textile, 1892, by Arthur Silver. Another good example of the influence of Japanese art on Silver Studio work.

26, Overleaf, left: Design for a furnishing textile circa 1890 by HW Batley. Batley often sold designs through the Silver Studio and this is a particularly charming example.

27, Overleaf, right: Design for a printed furnishing textile, 1890, by Arthur Silver. This shows the growing popularity of Oriental textile patterns for upholstery fabrics. The black background is particularly striking.

30 Design for a printed textile circa 1890 by Arthur Silver. An early example of Silver Studio's Art Nouveau, probably intended for Liberty's Art Fabrics range.

29, Right: Design for a wallpaper, 1894, by John Illingworth Kay. Art Nouveau designs such as this were becoming increasingly popular in middle-class homes at this time.

28, Far right: Design for a wallpaper, circa 1885 by Arthur Silver. This is a preliminary sketch for an exuberantly patterned pseudo rococo wallpaper.

SILVER STUDIO COLL.

PART·TWO: 1895-1910

EDWARDIAN·OPULENCE AND·NEW·ART

The kind of decoration described in the previous chapter continued to be popular for many years and the significant differences that were noticeable by about 1910 crept in gradually rather than as the result of a sudden change in fashion. But, at the same time, the years 1895-1910 did see a new and very different style of decorative art and interior decoration reaching the peak of its popularity. A modern style for the modern age and the new century, it was a deliberate reaction against the prevailing historical revivalism. Today we would call it Art Nouveau but at the time it was known as 'Modern', 'Quaint' or 'New Art'. 'Art Nouveau' was a derogatory term reserved for Continental and Scottish decorative art. One eminent English artist wrote:[1]

> 'I believe it is made on the Continent, and used by parents and others to frighten naughty children.'

In fact, English writers and designers had an immense and acknowledged effect on the development of Continental and American Art Nouveau; the importance of English work abroad is indicated by the fact that in the early 1900s more than half of the Silver Studio 'modern' designs were being sold to foreign manufacturers. Nevertheless, Continental Art Nouveau was written off as a decadent eccentricity and its elegant asymmetries were described as entrails and 'squirming lines and blobs'.

English New Art decoration ranged from the expensive simplicity of 'Arts and Crafts' to the more convoluted Quaint forms but its fabrics and wallpapers always used extremely stylized patterns, usually based on flowers, foliage or seed heads. Any attempt to copy nature directly or to produce 'imitation' effects was considered abhorrent and the Modern designs, whether the earlier productions with their sinuous lines and organic shapes or the later more restrained and formal patterns, were always non-naturalistic and two-dimensional.

Although as a generally available decorating style it really only got going in the 1890s, its beginnings stretched further back and further afield. The Arts and Crafts element in the New Art was very strong and the work of William Morris was particularly influential. He had expressed the view that the use of machinery and factory methods in the modern Victorian age was responsible for the appalling ugliness of most domestic goods and that factory conditions were degrading to the people who worked in them. He looked back to an age of the artist-craftsman, working honestly and lovingly to make objects of beauty. This idealization of the pre-industrial age led Morris to study historic patterns and forms and much of his work shows this old-world character. Unfortunately, his insistence on craftsmanship meant that most Morris goods were too expensive for ordinary people to buy. Nevertheless, his patterns and ideas had a great effect both on other designers and on public taste, especially during the 1880s and 90s, when interior decoration was becoming an increasingly widespread preoccupation. A number of architects, artists

1 Preceding pages: Cretonne c 1895. Many Silver Studio designs of this period were responsive to the popularity of the patterns of William Morris.

2, Right: Silver Studio design c 1910.

3 One of the friezes designed by Arthur
Silver for Rottman and Co. Stencilled on
Japanese grass paper it would form part of an
expensive New Art scheme. 1895.

and designers, following some, if not all of Morris's ideas and aesthetic values, formed a loosely knit group which came to be known as the Arts and Crafts Movement. Holding to the belief in 'truth to materials' and 'honest craftsmanship', their work tended to share a recognizable style. They set up several craft guilds, such as the Century Guild and the Artworkers' Guild, to produce decorative art, furniture, textiles and wallpaper. Although such goods were still rather expensive, the accompanying displays and publicity were able to reach a wide public and the general awareness of this kind of design was further increased by the annual shows of the Arts and Crafts Exhibition Society and by the publication of a number of popular arts magazines, the most well-known of which was the *Studio*.

The New Art emphasis on structural simplicity, flatness of pattern and elegance of line also owed something to the art of Japan. Popular 'Aesthetic' decoration of the 1880s and early 90s had crowded its rooms with Japanese fans, screens, pottery and panels painted with Orientally-inspired scenes but the New Art adapted rather than adopted Japanese motifs. The furniture, textiles and other decorative work of designers such as Christopher Dresser, EW Godwin and AH Mackmurdo, key figures in the birth of British Art Nouveau, show their interest in the formal clarity of Japanese designs. Particularly influential were the beautifully rhythmic, conventionalized patterns of woodblocks and stencils. Arthur Silver himself was deeply interested in Japanese art, subscribing to Bing's *Artistic Japan*, and collecting Japanese prints and stencil sheets. He also collaborated with Rottman & Co, importers of Japanese papers, on a venture to produce deep stencilled wall friezes on grass paper. So successful and innovatory was this that he was interviewed at length about it by the *Studio* magazine. Stencilling was often used in New Art wallcoverings and the strong outlines of the technique are also found in many designs that were block or roller printed.

The Silver Studio played an important part in the popularity of the new decorative style. Arthur Silver was a part of the group which was at the forefront of this fashion and was particularly close to important designers such as Walter Crane, Christopher Dresser and CFA Voysey (some of whose designs are still in the collection today). He showed work at the Arts and Crafts exhibitions from 1889 onwards. But perhaps even more importantly from the point of view of popularizing the style, he worked closely with nearly all of the leading manufacturers of the day. Originally the Arts and Crafts Movement had been opposed to machine manufacture, but when some of its ideas and styles were taken up by mass production they were brought within the reach of the less well off. Wallpaper firms such as Essex, Woollams and Jeffrey and Co produced very fine, characteristically modern papers. Some were hand printed and therefore reasonably expensive, but a good number were machine printed and could cost less than 1s 0d a piece (about eleven yards). Such firms were sufficiently in tune with Arts and Crafts ideas to use the best designers and to credit them in their publicity material.

This raised the status of wallpaper to something near art and was a useful marketing ploy at a time when 'artistic' was the main term of decorating approbation. For textiles, firms such as Liberty, Simpson & Godlee, and Warners were amongst Silver's best customers.

The first Silver Studio designs that were clearly Art Nouveau were produced in the early 1890s and from 1895 to about 1905 its output was almost entirely in this style. In the mid-1900s, when Rex and Harry Silver were running the studio after Arthur's death, it was selling about 300 designs a year. Produced both by 'high class' and more popular manufacturers in the UK, on the Continent and in the United States, the work of the studio was not only frequently featured in the art magazines but was very widely available both at home and abroad.

The interested public could see the Arts and Crafts style of decorating at its most pure in the pages of the *Studio* magazine. Established in 1893 and edited by Gleeson White, a close friend of Arthur Silver, the *Studio*, with its fine illustrations, reviews and design competitions, was a major expositor of New Art ideals and a showcase for its artefacts. It not only showed the new style but used a new way of presenting it. Instead of the compelling bossiness of Mrs Panton and the columns of the ladies' magazines, the *Studio's* high-quality sketches and photographs and accurate descriptions of real rooms and decorative items tempted its readers to emulation. This approach became increasingly common. *Country Life* (1896) and later magazines, such as *Homes and Gardens* used it as a matter of course. Perhaps the readers of such magazines were already so *au fait* with the niceties of interior decoration that, unlike Mrs Panton's newly arrived middle classes, they did not feel the need for detailed instructions. However, the ordinary person could hardly hope to copy exactly the houses and rooms shown, for they had often been specially designed for particular clients with everything, even down to the door fittings, organized as a complete scheme. This was a period when wealthy businessmen and manufacturers were building themselves houses in the country, within fairly easy reach of the town by train or motor car, which they could use for weekends and brief visits. The Arts and Crafts or 'domestic vernacular' style was particularly appropriate for such clients because it nicely combined the appearance of age and the suggestion of established country roots with modernity and a certain amount of informality.

The architects and designers of such houses tended to regard the conventional decoration of ordinary middle-class houses as irrational and pretentious. They felt that houses, already too small, were divided up into uselessly tiny rooms simply to satisfy the polite requirements of separate drawing-rooms, dining-rooms, morning-rooms, smoking-rooms and librar-ies. The ceilings of these poky little rooms were disproportionately high. Their large, plate-glass, sash windows served, not as might be thought, to admit light and air, but as showplaces for the conspicuous consumption of

4 Arts and Crafts dining-room designed by MH Baillie Scott, shown in *Modern British Domestic Architecture and Decoration*, 1901, a year-book of the *Studio* magazine. It would have been too extreme and expensive for the ordinary house but many of its features were adapted to more popular decorating.

5 Designs for dinner plates, c 1900. Only dessert and tea plates had decorated centres.

yards and yards of lace and elaborate draperies. Their mass of 'artistic' knick-knacks was vulgar and ugly. William Morris wrote in 1882:[2]

> 'Have nothing in your houses that you do not know to be useful, or believe to be beautiful.'

The 1890s saw an even wider expression of these views. CFA Voysey, for example, said:[3]

> 'Instead of painting boughs of apple trees on our door panels and covering every shelf with petticoats of silk, let us begin by discarding the mass of useless ornaments and banishing the millinery that degrades our furniture and fittings. Reduce the variety of patterns and colours in a room.'

We might find the sort of decoration that accompanied such ideas, often an elegant countrified simplicity, charming, but to people used to the kind of interiors described in the last chapter it seemed almost shockingly bare.

Arts and Crafts decoration could range from the medieval baronial to the cottagey or to the elegantly classical, but there were, throughout, certain common features. Low ceilings and lead-lighted casement windows, often with window-seats in the bay, combined to give an air of cosy domesticity. Good honest wood (usually oak or other English woods) was very evident in the polished or lightly stained floorboards, the panelled walls and the simple old English or modern furniture. The wood could be stained (green was a very popular colour for furniture) or plainly painted, especially in the drawing-room and bedrooms. Dark, multicoloured treatments and graining were not acceptable. Built-in furniture, clearly showing its wooden construction, was also common, with inglenooks in most rooms and built-in cupboards and wash-stands in the bedrooms. This not only produced the effect of reducing clutter but chimed in with the ever growing horror of dirt. Hygiene, especially in the bedrooms, was an increasing middle-class preoccupation and sedulous attempts were made to reduce the dust which was believed to harbour germs. Built-in furniture was one way of avoiding those rolls of fluff that tend to collect under wardrobes. (In the Arts and Crafts bedroom, however, the demands of craftsmanship and a homely appearance triumphed over hygiene. Although writers like Colonel Edis had for years been urging metal bedsteads on the grounds that their smooth surfaces offered no home for germs, New Art preferred wood.)

Rather than going for the approach in which every available space was a mass of pattern and detail, these rooms relied for their effect on limited areas of elaborate decoration and on contrasts of plain and pattern. The focal decorative point in the reception rooms was the fireplace. There was nothing new in that – but instead of a narrow built-in grate and tall crowded overmantel there would be a wide, welcoming, open hearth with firedogs or freestanding basket. Perhaps surrounded with glazed or hand-painted tiles, it was often topped with a glowing copper hood. With an alcove or inglenook and a motto of homely philosophy in olde-worlde script along the top, the fire's position at the heart of the home would be assured. Inlays of wood or metal (often beaten copper), large hinges or locks, perhaps more mottoes and panels of stained glass relieved the plainness of the furniture and fitments. The stamped leathers, woven doublecloths, printed velvets and cretonnes with their large, highly stylized swirling patterns could be striking and sumptuous in their colour and texture, but they were fitted closely to the chairs or the cushions on the wooden benches and settles. The refectory table that replaced the massive mahogany telescoping dining table was bereft of chenille and plush cloths. The loose covers, frills and fringes which, in most homes, formed a tribute to the upholsterer's art, were banished. Also gone were the pelmets and tails of heavy window draperies. In their place were simply gathered folds falling to the floor or window ledge with, perhaps, little casement curtains across the windows themselves. Scattered on the polished floors would be a few Oriental or modern rugs.

For simplicity's sake, the main wall divisions were now reduced to two, the break coming at about door height. The main wall area could be plain or patterned but panelling was particularly desirable, especially in the hall and dining-room. The rather deep frieze above was then colour-washed or filled with large patterning. The Rottman-Silver stencilled friezes mentioned earlier were ideal for this purpose. Frieze papers almost always had a horizontal thrust to the design to finish off the wall – even landscapes, trees and figures were treated in this way. MH Baillie Scott, one of the *Studio's* favourite architects, suggested a couple of colour schemes for the drawing-room: wallpaper in tones of golden-yellow and orange; yellowish-white woodwork and warm white furniture. The same tones would be picked up in the curtains, cushions and copper sconces and plaques. With green felt and an Oriental carpet on the floor, a piquant point of interest could be a single piece of furniture in stained green oak. Alternatively, with the whole room in tones of greeny-blue, white and purple, the contrast could be provided by a few pieces of bright orange pottery.

But, in spite of the 'modernity' of such decoration, many of the old accepted conventions remained in force. Although colours were in general lighter, halls and dining-rooms continued to receive a heavier, darker treatment than drawing-rooms and bedrooms and it was still considered absolutely essential to keep the servants and children as separate from the adult inhabitants and guests as space allowed. Nurseries might have their own special children's wallpapers and friezes, and bathrooms might just use decorative tiling and fitments, but the decoration of the service areas of the house – the kitchen, scullery and servants' quarters – owed more to function than to appearance.

Of course, these 'arty', completely-designed schemes were untypical and beyond the pocket of most people, however committed they might have

6 Fitted bedroom by Liberty and Co, c1900. The heavy patterning of the walls and fabrics contrasts with the white-painted woodwork.

7 Illustration from Waring and Gillow's catalogue showing reasonably priced green stained 'Quaint' furniture for the kitchen. It is only the detailing that makes this scheme New Art. In most respects it is similar to less fashionable kitchens.

8 Design for a printed textile, 1897.

9 This reconstruction of a small middle-class drawing-room, c 1900, at the Beamish North of England Open Air Museum shows a typical mixture of styles – draped mantelshelf, New Art upholstery fabric and 'Sheraton' furniture.

been to Arts and Crafts ideas. Nevertheless, it was quite possible to decorate in an authentic Arts and Crafts way using more widely available goods. Shops like Heals sold a range of simple well-made furniture on these lines and so did Liberty, which also specialized in fitted furniture, especially for bedrooms. Machine-made panelling in various finishes could be bought 'off-the-peg' in ranges with names such as 'Goehring' and 'Tudoresk'. But these things were still reasonably expensive. A fitted bedroom from Waring and Gillow would cost about £70 or £80 to equip completely and the cheaper panelling was about 1s 9d per square foot. This was rather a lot at a time when a reasonable white-collar salary might be about £200 or £300 a year. Another problem was that the vast majority of people did not own their own homes. Renting was the standard procedure and it was common to move

10 Soft greyish-blues were very popular. This
design dates from 1898.

much more frequently than we do today. It was therefore unwise to spend too much on items that might become 'landlord's fixtures' or which would not be adaptable to the next house.

However, for most people the New Art was more a decorative style than an act of faith and it was perfectly possible to buy inexpensive, mass-produced goods and to put together individual schemes with the help of the decorator and upholsterer. Furnishing catalogues and trade journals, such as *The Cabinet Maker And Art Furnisher*, (a wonderful source for discovering what was actually available to buy) showed the Quaint style simply as a popular alternative to the equally fashionable 'Sheraton', 'Chippendale' or 'Louis XVI'. The rather spartan effect of Arts and Crafts proper could be adapted according to available cash and individual taste, and it could be made more 'comfortable' by using more pattern and clutter. For example, wallpapers, which were used rather sparingly in the 'high' style, were immensely popular and the Silver Studio was kept very busy producing new designs for fillings and friezes.

Particularly in the popular market, there were changes in the style over the years. Mass-produced Quaint furniture of the mid-90s could be very quaint indeed, with a lot of curves and waving fretwork, but by about 1900 it tended to be rather simpler and more solid looking, often like proper Arts and Crafts pieces. Green staining, frequently with copper decoration and spade-shaped cut-outs, was wildly popular. There was a parallel change in the patterns used for textiles and wallpapers. The complicated, organically swirling designs and deep colours of the mid-90s gave way to simpler, more formally organized patterns and much lighter colours – soft blues, greens, mauves and pinks on pale grounds became popular.

It was possible to buy just about everything in the New Art style. Metalwork in particular was easily tortured into Art Nouveau shapes and it is still easy to find genuine examples of such things as finger plates, lamps, fire surrounds, coal baskets, fire-irons and vases. At the time, all these items could be combined in the conventional late Victorian manner. Green-stained furniture and copper hinges did not have to be accompanied by bare floorboards and refectory tables, they could equally well be used with portières, screens, dadoes and ornaments and for most people this must have been a more comfortable way of doing things. But it would be true to say that the New Art, or at least some of the ideas expressed in the New Art, did have a significant and lasting effect on the decoration of ordinary houses. The homely cottagey exteriors of the domestic vernacular were an inspiration for the standard form of early twentieth-century council housing and the traditional inter-war 'semi'. Interior decoration, even at its most nostalgic, has never returned to the crammed claustrophobia of the twilit, fringed and frilled late Victorian dining-room or drawing-room. The relatively empty rooms and light effects which were first seen in the New Art coincided with an ever increasing desire for cleanliness, sunlight and fresh

11 Illustration from Waring and Gillow's catalogue, c 1910. With its mahogany furniture, roses, stripes and light paintwork, this rather luxurious drawing-room is in an 'eighteenth-century English' style.

air and although dark or grained paint and dark colours certainly remained in use, the more upmarket styles of the twentieth century were never again as dark and cluttered as they had been.

This was true of the other fashionable decorating styles of the late 90s and early 1900s, for, although they were still based on the decoration of previous eras, the massive, heavily carved furniture and sombre tertiary colours of the 1880s and 90s were giving way to the less overwhelming eighteenth-century French and English furniture styles and to wallpapers, textiles and paintwork in light and pretty colours. It continued *de rigueur* to have a great deal of furniture. ('The indispensable furniture in a drawing-room consists of easy chairs and settees, occasional chairs, tea tables, a pianoforte, and one or two cabinets.'[4]) but the pieces themselves were smaller. The rather heavier forms of Chippendale and Queen-Anne remained widely available, but in the 1900s it was Sheraton that was particularly fashionable. With a satinwood finish and inlaid with delicate shell or star motifs of coloured wood, it had slender, straight tapering legs. In the same way, Louis XVI was preferred to the curves of Louis XV. Even 'Jacobean' oak (much used in dining-rooms) was treated in a less ebullient way. For the most part, such furniture was still very much 'in the style of ... ', but accuracy of reproduction and even a taste for the real thing was encouraged, paradoxically, by the Arts and Crafts reverence for old workmanship and by the increasing availability of photographs of genuine antiques shown in magazines such as *Country Life*. It was no longer smart to hide tables under shawls and cloths and the brocades, damasks, or tapestries which were used

12, Far left: French woven silks designed by the Silver Studio. Such fabrics were used for the upholstery in 'Louis' or 'Sheraton' rooms in the 1900s.

13, Left: A luxurious 'Louis' scheme, shown in *The Book of the Home*, 1906.

for upholstery revealed the outlines of the sofas and chairs, unmarred by frills and antimacassars.

To be absolutely correct, wallpapers and fabrics had to be in a style consistent with the furniture. 'Adams' or English florals went with eighteenth-century English furniture. Walls and curtains bloomed with lusciously pretty cabbage roses, lilac, wisteria and sweet peas on trellis-work or stripes of imitation moiré or lace bloomed on the walls and curtains. (These flowers were also very much in vogue in the gardens of the time where herbaceous borders and 'cottage garden' planting were replacing the stiffly formal and garish bedding arrangements of the mid-Victorian period.) Colours were soft pinks, blues and greens on a white or very pale grey ground. Instead of a dado or frieze it was common, especially with a moiré or stripe, to have a border of flowers around the top of the wall or to use narrow floral strips to form panel shapes. Some manufacturers made chintzes and cretonnes to match the papers exactly and these were used for curtains and loose covers. The woodwork to accompany such schemes would usually be white or cream. French-style rooms were not dissimilar though the patterns might show pale blue or green ribbons and pearl ropes linking the roses or romantic little groups of musical instruments and gardening tools or tiny 'empire' laurel wreaths. A mirror or picture replaced the high, shelved overmantel and the venetian or roller blinds at the window were

14 A slightly 'old-fashioned' treatment for the hall suggested in *The Book of the Home*, 1906. The drapery and the fern in an 'art' pot serve to draw attention from the upper part of the stairs and the back of the passageway.

15, Above right: In areas where hard wear or hygiene were especially important it was common to use a wallpaper varnished to a washable finish. The warm, rather dark colours of this example from about 1900 would have been especially useful for a hallway.

disappearing, although there were still quite elaborate arrangements for the curtains and pelmets.

The lampshades were often marvellously frilly confections which had the added advantage of softening the rather harsh effect of the electric light that was becoming usual in many well-to-do households.

Schemes like these were found in the drawing-room, but rather quieter and less luxurious versions might also be used in boudoirs or bedrooms for the ladies. A constant theme of writers on home decoration was that bedroom papers should on no account have the kind of patterns that 'grow annoying when they have to be contemplated during the long feverish hours of an invalid's day'. Floral chintzes and cretonnes were much used and the toilet-ware might well be in complementary patterns. Bedroom furniture was customarily bought in matching suites comprising bed, wardrobe, dressing table, and at least a couple of chairs. A wash-stand was usually included even though, by this time, all new middle-class houses were built with bathrooms.

In contrast to such very feminine rooms, halls, dining-rooms and libraries used heavier fabrics, deeper colours and more solid furniture. The main decorative considerations for the hall were to give a 'cosy' first impression of the house and to stand up to hard wear. For the latter reason, dadoes continued in common use and this also applied in dining-rooms. Wainscott was the preferred material but if this was not possible, tough materials like Lincrusta were acceptable. It was still not quite 'proper' to allow visitors a clear view of the stairs or the back part of the hall leading to the kitchen and an archway or curtains served as a notional screen. Blues and

CANDLE SHADES.

C H 207.
Parchment Empire Trimmed Ribbon and Chenille, 1/1 each. (All colors)

C H 3493.
Embroidered Silk in Pink, White, Yellow or Green Grounds, 2/4 each.

C H 5512.
Empire Parchment Trimmed Ribbons, Gold Sequins and Chenille, 1/4½ each. (All colors).

C H 3843.
Chene Silk Empire Coloring only as shown, 3/4 each.

C H 5506.
Parchment Empire Panels of Gold Sequins and Pink Roses, 1/2½ each, all colored ground.

C H 2398.
Silk Petal Clip on Shade. in all Colors, 1/3½ each.

C H 121.
Silk Petal Clip, on Shade, 11¼d. each. In all colors.

C H 743.
Electric Gimbal with swivel fittings, Sarsnet Silk, lined white. In all colors, 3/6 each.

C H 2400.
Silk Petal Clip on Shade, in all colors, 1/3¼ each.

C H 221.
Silk Petal Clip on Shade, with linen roses and leaves, Pink, Yellow & Red, 1/6½ each.

C H 7832.
Empire Parchment Shade, Floral Chintz decoration, best quality, picture,
| 10 | 12 | 14 | 18 | 22 in. |
| 7/9 | 11/9 | 13/9 | 17/9 | 22/9 |

C H 5303.
Glazed Linen collapsible Shade, Hand Painted,
| 12 | 14 | 16 in. deep |
| 7/6 | 8/9 | 11/6 |

C H 7819.
Parchment Shade, real Empire design, trimmed Green Chenille,
| 10 | 12 | 14 | 18 | 22 in. |
| 13/3 | 15/6 | 20/9 | 25/- | 32/- |

C H 32540.
White Chene Broche Silk Lamp Shade,
| 14 | 16 | 18 | 20 | 22 in. |
| 16/6 | 19/6 | 22/- | 27/6 | 31/6 |

C H 696583.
Painted Silk Shade with Bead Fringe, Pink or White Ground,
| 14 | 16 | 18 | 20 in. |
| 25/6 | 29/9 | 33/6 | 38/9 |

C H 696582.
Painted Silk Empire Shade, Bead Fringe, Pink or White Ground,
| 14 | 16 | 18 | 20 in. |
| 21/6 | 24/- | 26/9 | 33/6 |

HARRODS Ltd.

C H 2998.
Silk and Chiffon Shade trimmed with Hand made Lace, 21 in. 26/-.

C H 3000.
Silk and Chiffon Shade trimmed with Hand made Lace, 22 in. 22/6.

16 Such shades had been in use for many years and went with most kinds of decoration.

17 Illustration from Hampton and Sons catalogue, c 1905, showing a bedroom decorated in the eighteenth-century style.

greens or warm orangey-reds and yellows and soft browns were usual in both halls and dining-rooms and, especially in the dining-room, the paintwork did not have to be very light. For the hall there were rugs, matting or carpet strips which could easily be taken up and shaken, but a good carpet, Turkey or Wilton by choice, was required in the dining-room, not only for its appearance but to deaden the clatter of knives and forks and the noise of the servants as they moved about. Although the general tone of the dining-room was one of beefy masculinity, the table decorations for formal dinners with their little flower bowls, trails of ribbon or leaves and elaborate centre-pieces offered great scope for feminine ingenuity.

'Ideal' schemes such as these were a progression, rather than an abrupt change, from the immediately previous ways of decorating. They were upmarket and urban and it would be quite wrong to suggest that they were universal even amongst the middle classes. The most expensive silk brocade could cost £15 a yard and even the cheaper brocades at about 6s must have been beyond the reach of many. On £500 a year, a family could afford a 'respectable' London address and keep three servants, but in 1901 only 400,000 people earned more than £400 per annum. Apart from the cost of the goods themselves, it would take the efforts of a number of servants and

18 A living-room in a new block of council flats in London, 1901. This very Victorian kind of decoration did not disappear for many years.

frequent redecoration to counteract the effects of incessant coal-dust on white moiré finish paper. 'Edwardian' is a byword for opulence and luxury, but many people, even the ever increasing number who commanded a reasonable middle-class income, continued to enjoy their dark grained paintwork, their varnished hall papers, hard-wearing dadoes, their antimacassars and mantelshelf draperies for many more years.

NOTES

1 George Frampton, RA, quoted in 'L'Art Nouveau, what it is and what is thought of it. A Symposium', *Magazine of Art*, 1904.
2 William Morris, *Hopes and Fears for Art*, 1882, p 108.
3 Quoted in the *Studio*, Vol I, 1893, p 234.
4 HJ Jennings, *Our Homes and How to Beautify Them*, 1902, p 183.

19 This turn-of-the-century drawing-room has most of the features of the New Art style – low frieze rail, large patterned paper, light woodwork, a motto and a Quaint overmantel with ornamental hinges – but it is much less austere than the Arts and Crafts room seen in illustration 4.

20 This woven wool tapestry of 1898 with its hard-edged stylized thistles and acanthus leaves is a typical Silver Studio design. Manufactured by the French company, Leborgne, it was a rather expensive upholstery fabric.

21 Design for wallpaper, 1899. Illustration 19 shows a room decorated with an almost identical paper. Patterns, especially for carpets and wallpapers, could be quite enormous. Some writers on interior decoration asserted that a large pattern increased the apparent size of a small room.

22, Above: A fine example of a deep, large-scale frieze paper. It was made by Shand Kydd and cost 3s 6d a yard. Poppies were often used in Studio designs of this period.

23 This charming design by Harry Silver is typical of the simpler New Art patterns which were popular in the early 1900s. It is clearly influenced by the work of CFA Voysey.

24, *Above:* An elegant, formal design of stylized thistles for a printed furnishing textile, c 1905.

25, *Centre:* Art Nouveau furnishing fabrics were severely fitted. Prominent upholstery studs added to the uncompromising effect. Cheap ranges of furniture in this style were available from the mid-90s onwards.

26, *Right:* Wallpaper, c 1905, with a simple Arts and Crafts pattern.

27 Design for a ceiling paper, 1895. It was conventional to graduate the colours in a room from floor to ceiling, the palest at the top.

28, Left: Design for a woven silk for the drawing-room, c1905.

29, Above: Silver Studio designed woven wool tapestry, 1908.

30, Left: 'Roses and ribbons' for a printed textile, 1905.

31, Above right & right: 'Jacobean' cretonnes, adapted to the prevailing taste in colour and style, have been popular throughout the twentieth century. This design, c 1905, would have been used in a dining-room or an Old English country drawing-room.

32, Above: Wallpaper design, 1903. A French pattern like this would be used without a frieze.

33, Centre: Pretty florals were much in vogue for bedrooms. Bedspread design, 1908.

34, Right: Silver Studio design, 1907. Chintzes were used for loose covers and curtains in drawing-rooms and bedrooms.

PART·THREE: 1910-1925

IN·PRAISE·OF·ENGLISH PAST

The years around the First World War brought some fundamental changes in approach to household organization and decoration. Victorian taste was by now regarded by most writers on decoration as horrendously old-fashioned. Even books for that usually very conservative being, the professional painter and decorator, shuddered at the memory of marbled hallways, rampant patterning, overdressed windows and multi-coloured woodwork. And only a dozen years after the death of Edward VII it was said that:[1]

> 'We are no longer ruled by the passion for white paint that possessed some decorators of the Edwardian period; ivory and pale cream tints no longer adorn every wall … '

This was partly a straightforward reaction against the tastes of the immediately preceding generation but it also registered a recognition that Victorian and Edwardian conventions of household organization and decoration had perhaps never been entirely appropriate for the way that many people were obliged, or even wished, to live. The well-to-do could afford formality and luxury. They had the space to keep some rooms apart for visitors; to keep their servants and children out of sight; to make distinctions between the male and female areas of the house; and to decorate all these rooms accordingly. But to attempt to do all this with only two reception rooms and perhaps three or four bedrooms was impossible. In 1913 one writer put it this way:[2]

> 'People in moderate circumstances whose income is derived from work are finding that it is neither comfortable nor dignified to attempt to reproduce in their own homes the domestic environment of the leisured wealthy.'

With a general relaxation of the strict Victorian and Edwardian codes of behaviour, such people were turning to styles which suggested informality, cosiness and simplicity rather than ceremonious affluence. And, especially after the war, they were joined by the previously comfortable who, hit by the shortages of goods, the difficulty of getting servants, the higher cost of living and rates of tax, were dubbed the 'nouveau poor'.

Inside and out, houses were beginning to reflect these changing attitudes. The majority of late Victorian and Edwardian houses were in fact suburban although their layout, if not their facade, derived from the urban Georgian terrace. But there was an increasing desire for a more rural effect and, even as far back as the 1870s, there had been some interest in planning suburban estates which suggested villages rather than city streets. The early twentieth century saw a terrific interest in genuine country cottages and, encouraged by new magazines like *Homes and Gardens* (1919) and *Ideal Home* (1922), it was very desirable to own and restore the real article. New houses too were beginning to show olde-worlde cottagey characteristics. In the 1900s the 'advanced' domestic vernacular houses of Hampstead Garden

1, Preceding pages: Printed textile, c 1925.

2 This living-hall scheme of 1913 evokes a
traditional English past. The smaller
decorative items, such as the light fittings and
ornaments, are in keeping with the oak
furniture, beamed walls and open hearth.

3 Although genuinely old country cottages were very desirable, many people preferred new houses which combined modern materials and facilities with the appearance of age. This advertisement for a floor-covering from Liberty shows the kind of effect to aim for.

Suburb were set amongst greens, winding roads, and a generally leafy aspect. While such Garden Suburbs had originally been viewed rather as the ideal habitat for eccentric, 'artistic' types, more and more ordinary spec-built houses began to take up some of these elements. They were now often semi-detached rather than terraced, with roughcast walls and timbering and frequently featured tiled rather than slate roofs and casement, not sash, windows.

The Victorian terraced house usually had a back extension which, on the ground floor, housed the kitchen and scullery. While it had the advantage of keeping these rooms rather separate from the living accommodation, it did overshadow the back rooms and meant that access to the garden was down the narrow and often windy yard at the side. The new houses tended to do away with the back extension, bringing a combined kitchen-scullery into the main body of the house and giving direct access to, and a good view of, the garden from the back rooms. This more compact plan gave a lighter and cosier effect. In the more substantial kind of house there was something of a vogue for the living-hall. Entered from the front door, usually from a lobby or vestibule, this room served as a combination of some or all of dining-room, sitting-room, reception room and passageway, often actually replacing one of these rooms. Even for houses where there was no living-hall as such it was increasingly recognized that many people did, in fact, use their drawing-rooms or, more commonly, their dining-rooms as general purpose family rooms and because of this the more informal 'sitting-room' began to replace the term 'drawing- room'.

Decorating schemes developed in a similar direction. The more luxurious fashions of the previous decade suffered a decline and it was said of the French styles in particular:[3]

> ... suited as they were to the very formal and ceremonial periods in which they were produced, and of which they were reflections, they are something of an anachronism in our present unconventional and democratic age, and their use should be greatly restricted.'

What were really popular now were the English seventeenth- and eighteenth-century styles. 'Tudor' and 'Jacobean' decoration especially was felt to give a suitably simple, countrified, cottagey effect and its evocation of an old English past chimed in well with the rampant nationalism of the period.

It was a style for all classes and pockets. Those on tighter incomes could buy unashamedly new Jacobean furniture and often did so on hire purchase in spite of the constant warnings of the decorating manuals against the big advertising 'cash or credit' firms, who used slogans like 'You marry the girl and we furnish the home'. Such furniture was often bought in suites, the individual pieces somewhat scaled down to suit small rooms. The well-to-do could pick up original pieces or could buy accurate reproductions from firms like Gill and Reigate. They preferred to mix their styles a little. Genuine

Tudor and Jacobean furniture didn't come in matching sets and very period schemes, like that of EF Benson's snobbish heroine, Mrs Emmeline Lucas, were considered rather pretentious:[4]

> ' … here was … the famous smoking parlour, with rushes on the floor, a dresser ranged with pewter tankards, and leaded latticed windows of glass so antique that it was practically impossible to see out of them. It had a huge open fire-place framed in oak beams, with a seat on each side of the iron-backed hearth within the chimney, and an iron spit hung over the middle of the fire. Here, though in the rest of the house she had, for the sake of convenience, allowed the installation of electric light, there was no such concession made, and the sconces on the wall held dim iron lamps, so that only those of the most acute vision were able to see to read. Even to them reading was difficult, for the bookstand on the table contained nothing but a few crabbed black-letter volumes dating from not later than the early seventeenth century, and you had to be in a frantically Elizabethan frame of mind to be at ease there. But Mrs Lucas often spent rare leisure moments there, playing on the virginal that stood in the window, or kippering herself in the smoke of the wood-fire as with streaming eyes she deciphered an Elsevir Horace, rather late for inclusion under the rule, but an undoubted bargain.'

Collecting a few good old pieces, even if they were of different periods, was a more acceptable way of going about it. Jacobean furniture was in any case horribly uncomfortable and it was quite usual to include a few later items, maybe a grandfather chair or some chintz-covered easy chairs.

This style was most frequently used in halls, country sitting-rooms, sitting-halls and dining-rooms, and with the need for rooms to be more adaptable, it was the smaller, easily shifted pieces of furniture that were particularly popular. A gate-leg table which could be folded and placed out of the way was a ubiquitous feature of both sitting- and dining-rooms. Dining tables lost their time-honoured place in the middle of the room – they were more out of the way in a recess or window bay. Cries of horror arose at the enormous sideboard of the Victorian era:[5]

> 'It is something of a fetish … What on earth is the use of that big sheet of plate-glass, that lofty carved cornice, and those flanking Corinthian columns? … We feel a little overwhelmed, a little bullied and overpowered, by the gigantic piece of furniture which impels us to be solemn and dignified at dinner, as if we were eating in a church.'

It was replaced by an oak dresser whose shelves displayed books, old china or a collection of pewter. There might be room for a Chesterfield or a couple of lounge chairs which, like the dining chairs, would be covered with leather or, if that was too expensive, Rexine, at a quarter the cost. In the sitting-room the extreme hardness of Jacobean settles could be mitigated by the use of velvet-covered cushions, but for the most part the really uncomfortable seating was relegated to the hall.

1. Chinese Decoration
2. Patterned Dado and Border with plain filling
3. Panelling effects by patterned borders on plain papers
4. Panelling effect in dark oak paper on distemper wall. Deal cornice covered with oak paper
5. Imitation Oak Dado: wall and frieze in distemper
6. Tapestry Paper framed in real or imitation oak

WALL DECORATION

4 It was common to break up the wall surface with decorative borders or panelling. These examples, from *The Book of the Home*, 1925, are quite straightforward but it was also possible to produce more complicated schemes.

The narrow passage hallway of most houses had always been rather difficult to deal with satisfactorily. Ideally it should both be an entrance and a reception area but lack of space meant that its grand origins in the medieval manor house could only be hinted at. Decorating writers nagged constantly about cutting down on furniture:[6]

'Make a clean sweep of antlers, spears, assegais, shields and all other miscellaneous animal relics and weapons of warfare which can never properly be seen, and which make an already small and poky place appear more crowded and more stuffy.'

But at a time when everybody wore hats and most people carried umbrellas, some sort of provison for these was necessary. The best answer was to provide a separate cloakroom or a hall cupboard but the more usual solution was a Jacobean stand which joined the barometer and monk's bench (the back folded down to make a table) or chest just inside the front door.

5 An example of imitation tapestry wallpaper. Such papers were used mainly in dining-rooms and halls, often in the form of panels. After The First World War soft greys and purples were more popular than the previous greens.

Dark brown (on no account white) woodwork went with oak furniture. Generally the colours were rather low toned, although the ceiling and frieze, especially if one were lucky enough to have a beamed ceiling, was usually distempered white. It was common practice to add a dash of colour to the distemper – blue for a bright white effect or one of the colours used on the walls for a warmer feeling. Real oak panelling was highly prized, but for those who could not manage this there were plenty of ways of getting the right effect. Lincrusta, for instance, imitated solid panelling. A simple form of skeleton panelling could be easily and cheaply achieved with strips of deal, dark painted or grained and nailed to the wall, or with moulded or patterned paper borders or even simply with painted outlines. The next step was to add pieces of tapestry or, much more likely, an imitation. In the years before the war there was a huge range of tapestry wallpapers to choose from. Some were rather simple, often diaper patterns, printed on textured paper and given a stitchy treatment, while others were wonderful scenic productions

6 Advertisement for 'Devon' fires, c 1920. The one at the top is rather Georgian, the other neo-Tudor.

showing forests and stags and ruined castles in the marvellously gloomy blues and greens of the faded hangings seen in old country houses. In the early 1920s such papers were still available but the colouring tended to be softer, more grey and mauve, and there was a growing fashion for using plainer papers or paint in soft warm-toned colours. The heavily patterned tapestry papers were too overwhelming to use in large areas and they were usually broken up by the skeleton panelling frames or were applied in panel-shaped pieces, finished with a narrow border, on a plain ground.

Fabrics were in keeping. There were Jacobean embroidery or chintz patterns and cretonnes with soft but heavy allover designs of flowers, foliage and birds. In the pre-war years the prevailing colours were rather dark, with a lot of blues and greens, quite often on a black ground, but in the early 20s a lighter brighter effect was more general. There would be simple casement curtains, perhaps loose covers on some of the chairs, and for a truly cottagey effect, a valance along the top of the brick, wood or stone chimney opening.

By this time electric lighting was no longer a novelty and people were beginning to pay more attention to its decorative use. It was generally felt that diffused light, directed at the ceiling or walls and reflected back into the room, gave a particularly pleasant effect. Wall sconces were given silk or parchment baffle shades, bulbs could be fitted into the cornice moulding and pendant bowl fittings became almost ubiquitous. These, suspended from chains or cords, were generally of alabaster or opaque glass but some, specially suitable for the 'Tudorbethan' room, were of wood. Also in style were iron lantern pendants (with yellowish glass to give a pleasant glow) for the hall, candlestick fitments of all kinds and torch brackets with flame-shaped glass globes.

Smarter, more formal, drawing-rooms used the eighteenth-century styles, with Queen-Anne, Sheraton, Chippendale or Hepplewhite furniture. They too employed a panelling effect. There might well be a rather low dado with the wall space above divided up into rectangular areas by narrow mouldings or by borders of paper or paint. These panels were usually placed vertically but the arrangement could be as complicated as the ingenuity of the decorator allowed. A restrained treatment would simply pick out the mouldings or borders in a different colour but it was also popular to use a strong pattern inside the panels in contrast with a plainer treatment of the stiles.

This was not a period when foreign design was generally popular, but Chinese patterns, with their long pedigree of use in England, were the exception. These wallpapers and textiles with charming patterns of exotic birds and flowers were very fashionable and were particularly useful for Georgian schemes. Because of the lively colours of such patterns people were advised to restrict their use, either to halls and bedrooms, which were not in constant use, or to smaller areas in rooms which were frequently occupied. This was even more necessary when such patterns were printed

7 A low, painted, panelled dado, an
eighteenth-century fireplace and glass-
fronted fitted cupboards in the alcoves form
the basis of this 'Georgian' drawing-room of
the early 1910s.

on a black ground. For a while extremely fashionable, these papers and fabrics were strikingly smart but they would have easily become overwhelming. Whereas the late Victorians liked to contrast pattern with pattern it was by now conventional wisdom that a heavy pattern should be used in contrast with plain. Fashionable colours were pale Georgian greens and greys and shades of mauve with the white or light green woodwork that was felt to complement mahogany furniture.

This generally more reticent approach extended also to the window draperies of even the more formal kind of rooms. The heavy curtains hung straight to the floor behind a flat pelmet, perhaps with a sculpted edge and constrasting trimming and, instead of the elaborate protruding cornice of the Victorian window, they were arranged within the architrave. For a similarly elegant effect, fitted cupboards, with open or glass fronts, were made to look like niches by continuing the line of the wall above and below the shelves.

These styles were popular before the war and continued so afterwards, Tudorbethan in particular, mixed and matched with the currently fashionable wallpapers and fabrics, remaining a perennial favourite right through the 1920s and 30s. But during the war itself decorating was not a high priority. With severe rationing, tragic personal losses, and shortages of goods and labour, people had other things to occupy them. Wallpaper manufacturers issued only very limited new ranges. Furniture was in very short supply. Painters and decorators were away at the front and certain essential decorating materials were hard to come by. Wallpaper paste, for example, was unobtainable because it was largely composed of flour, now necessary for food. Hardly any new British books on interior decorating were published between 1914 and 1920. Nevertheless, the Silver Studio itself was very busy for most of the war years, helped by the demand for textiles from the United States which was now dependent on Britain as communications with France and Germany had been cut off. However, conscription took five of the fifteen designers and apprentices and when, in 1917, Rex Silver himself was called up the Silver Studio closed for over a year and did not regain its former strength until 1920.

After the war many people were faced with a pressing question that had a lasting effect on household organization: how to manage without servants. This need arose partly because there were fewer people willing or able to go into service. Men had been lost in the war and for girls there were other respectable jobs increasingly available in the growing clerical and light industrial fields which offered them more freedom than they could hope for in service. Nor could people afford servants so easily. Prices had risen sharply and took time to fall back. Rates of tax were increased. And although more and more people were achieving a reasonable income it was not enough to sustain a household staff at pre-war levels.

With the housewife having to do more of her own work, magazines and books abounded in labour-saving hints and promoted labour-saving

8 Wallpaper, c 1920.

9 In the 1920s many books and magazines offered advice on how to manage without servants and how to cut down on housework. This picture is taken from *The Servantless House*. Door furniture would be painted black and steps would be left alone except for the occasional scrub. Although the door is painted white it was much more common for external woodwork to be dark green or brown.

10, *Above right:* The new kitchen cabinets were smaller than the traditional dressers and were sold as being more efficient.

equipment. The kitchen was the main target. Gas and electric cookers, clean and easy to maintain, were replacing solid fuel kitcheners and ranges. Space-saving kitchen cabinets such as the 'Quicksey', with specially designed storage fitments, pull-out table tops and enclosed cupboards were taking over from the old open-shelved dressers. Some of the really time consuming items and methods began to disappear. Front steps were reddened weekly rather than whitened daily. Wood and oxidized or painted iron took the place of brass for items such as stair rods and door furniture. Mechanical and electric appliances, which before the war had been used by servants to help them do their work better if not more quickly (very early vacuum cleaners were worked by two people), were now sold as labour-saving devices. The advent of mechanical carpet sweepers encouraged a slight resurgence of fitted carpets, circumventing the old arguments about the difficulty of cleaning them.

There was still a very heavy schedule of housework, with fires to light, hand washing, fewer convenience foods and daily shopping, but ever since this time ease of maintenance has been an important factor in the way we manage and decorate our houses and marks the strong difference between Victorian and Edwardian methods.

These were deep-seated and long-lasting responses to the changed conditions which had become established during the war. But a more immediate and short-lived reaction to the bleakness of those years was the blaze of colour and exotic pattern which came to a head in the early 20s.

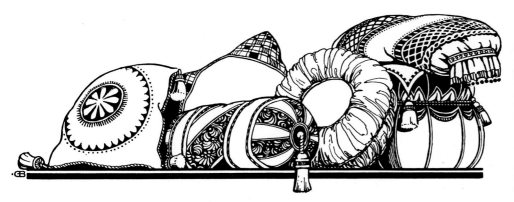

Numerous suburban sitting-rooms called upon the romance of a loosely interpreted East. The discovery of the tomb of Tutankamun in 1922 seized the public imagination; there was a passion for novels with exotic settings; and cinemas, themselves often resplendent Oriental palaces, showed films like the enormously popular *The Sheik*.

John Galsworthy describes the drawing-room of the young, avant-garde and very wealthy Fleur Forsyte just after the war:[7]

> ' … with ivory panels, a copper floor, central heating, and cut-glass lustres. It contained four pictures – all Chinese – … The fireplace, wide and open, had Chinese dogs with Chinese tiles for them to stand on. The silk was chiefly of jade green. There were two wonderful old black tea-chests … There was no piano, partly because pianos were too uncompromising occidental, and partly because it would have taken up too much room.'

She had tea at a little red lacquer table, her little Chinese dog, Ting-a-ling, completing the ensemble.

A less wealthy but still affluent and rather artistic sitting-room might have gold walls, black and gold silk curtains and exotic silk brocade-covered easy chairs. Others could use the many fabrics and wallpapers with modern adaptations of Oriental scenes. There were Chinese trees and islands, sunshades and lanterns in combinations of black and startlingly brilliant reds,

11, Above: After the austerity of the war years there was a move towards strong colours and a touch of the exotic.

12 & 13 There was a craze for richly decorated cushions and 'Chinese temple' lampshades.

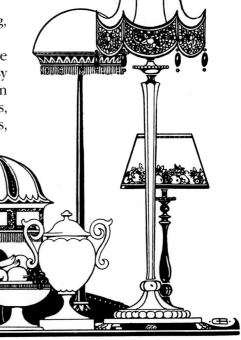

14 Design for a printed textile, 1925.

blues and oranges. Without going as far as Fleur Forsyte, people used these patterns together with their eighteenth-century furniture or their modern easy and bergere chairs. There were any number of smaller decorative items to give an exotic effect to an ordinary room. Divans, covered with black silk or Oriental shawls, had quite a vogue as did the glamorous cushions with which they would be piled. Round, triangular, oblong or bolster shaped, these cushions, made of silk, satin or brocade, much betrimmed and betasselled with metal galons and appliqué work, were strewn around, their borders and tassels languidly dangling à la desert tent. The great thing about such cushions was that anyone with a little skill and ingenuity could assemble them from scraps of rich-looking fabrics and trimmings. There were lacquer-work ornaments and furniture, small boxes and cocktail cabinets. There were parchment lampshades with tassels, bells, or chains of beads festooned from angle to angle, echoing the lines of Chinese pagodas and temples. Bonsai and miniature gardens were in vogue and the ferns and aspidistras of the Victorians were thrown out to make way for cacti, little glass trees and Oriental arrangements of branches in Chinese vases.

15 'Modern' cottage decoration often used painted furniture, strong colours and a variety of stripes and checks.

The rage for using knock-out colours combined with black was mainly a post-war phenomenon but it began in a small way rather earlier. In 1913 the Omega workshops opened up, selling a range of brightly coloured hand-painted furniture, decorative bits and pieces, hand-printed fabrics and clothes. Organized by Roger Fry and employing artistic talents like Duncan Grant, Vanessa Bell, Wyndham Lewis and Edward Wadsworth, the Omega was much influenced by Continental post-impressionist art and by Poiret's Atelier Martine which had opened in Paris in 1912 producing a similar range of brilliantly coloured items. Modern theatrical and ballet productions were also inspirational – the Ballet Russe with its exciting sets and brilliant costumes had burst upon London in 1912 and visited again in 1918. The Omega was able to take advantage of the gap for avant-garde design which had been opened up by the disappearance of Continental design during the war. However it only ever had a very small group of customers (mainly, it seems, connections of the Bloomsbury group) and with its erratic production methods, it only survived until 1919.

Since the decline of the Arts and Crafts movement, English modern design had been in the doldrums and although the Design and Industries Association was set up in 1915 in an attempt to remedy this, it seems to have had little effect. There were, however, some manufacturers, notably Foxtons, who were producing very good modern printed textiles. Stylistically, these had developed along similar lines to Continental Art Nouveau. Many designs featured little overall abstract patterns while others, known as Futurist, used French-inspired, flat, stylized groups or baskets of flowers, often on a checked or striped ground. Such designs, together with a range of more simple stripes and checks, usually exploited heavy, bright blues, yellows, emerald greens and pinkish reds, again with a great deal of black. Minnie

16 Design for printed textile, 1919. These colours are typical of avant-garde fabrics and wallpapers of the time.

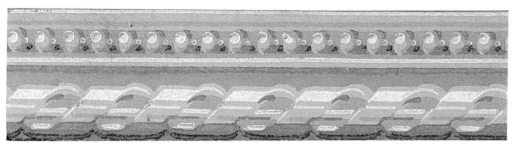

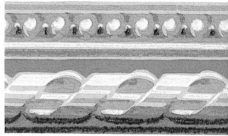

McLeish, C Mackintosh, Claud Lovat Frazer and Constance Irving were some of the designers who worked in this style and the Silver Studio too produced a number of Futurist designs in the years just after the war. These were sold to Foxtons, Story and Co and Fairfield Franklin.

Heal's was the sort of shop that stocked these fabrics, to complement its own range of furniture which, in direct line from the Arts and Crafts, was generally rather simple and clean-cut in shape. While it often employed high-quality woods and workmanship, there was also a vogue for 'cottage' style furniture painted in the prevailing blacks, greys and bright solid colours. For a sophisticated informal effect, avant-garde taste would combine this with colourful textiles, little check borders and decorative pottery against a plain, though still reasonably strongly coloured, background.

Wallpaper borders, available in all styles and colours, were perhaps the most ubiquitous decorative feature of this period. At their most simple they were narrow (about 1½ in) patterned bands with straight edges which were applied around the room below the picture rail or at ceiling level. They were also used just above the skirting and around the outside of the windows and door frames. A more complicated scheme would run these borders up the joins of a plain background paper and up the corners of the room. Yet more elaborate would be vertical or horizontal panels, with either simple mitred corners or more complicated angles. Cut-out borders with one or both sides cut to follow the edge of the pattern were also beginning their long run of

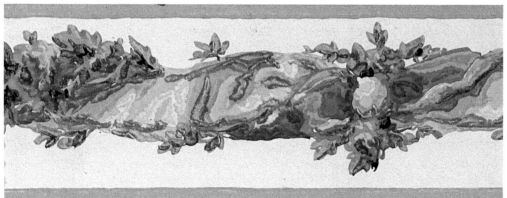

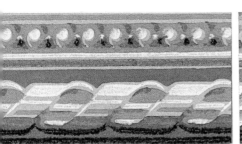 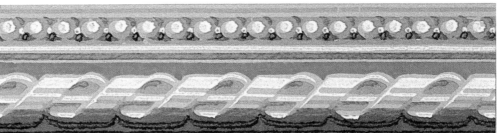

popularity and, increasingly elaborate, were beginning to take over from scenic friezes. Borders were used in all parts of the house: floral effects in the bedrooms; wider nursery borders and friezes at eye height under a ceiling paper with patterns of clouds or stars for children's rooms; and in the bathroom a blue and white border might outline varnished tile pattern panels on a crackle finish ground.

The versatility of these borders was especially useful as taste moved towards paler, softer, plainer, wall colours. The vogue for brilliant colours and strong patterns, whether 'Futurist', 'jazz effect' or 'semi-Orient', did not last very long. By 1921 such a decorative approach was being, perhaps a little prematurely, written off:[8]

> '[After the war] styles and modes gained currency which could never have enjoyed even a momentary vogue in normal times – *bizarre* fashions of an ugliness so crude that no producer or distributor would ever have dared formerly to foist them upon the public. Blaring, staring colour-schemes held the field of popularity such as could never have been tolerated in the older days … Purveyors of every kind of art material, whether textile or generally decorative, deliberately let go all hold on the buoys of rationality and went swirling off downstream on the turgid flood.'

This is a very negative response to a period of considerable liveliness but it is certainly true that by the mid-20s these eye-catching designs were a thing of the past.

17, Above, below & overleaf: Wallpaper borders, c 1925. Available in many styles, they could be used to provide a wide variety of effects.

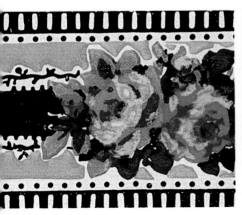 

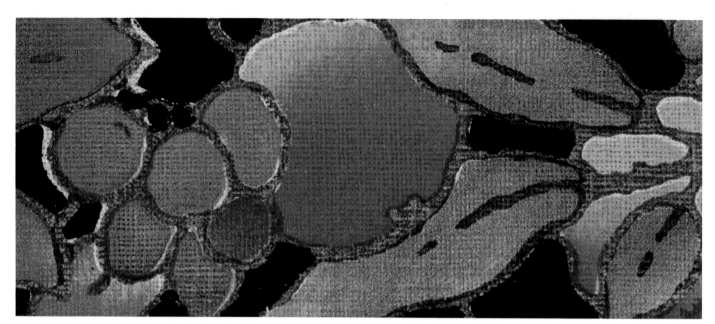

NOTES

1 John Gloag, *Simple Schemes for Decoration*, London, 1922, p 91.
2 EW Gregory, *The Art and Craft of Home Making*, London, 1913, p vi.
3 JH Elder-Duncan, *The House Useful and Beautiful. Being practical suggestions on furnishing and decoration*, London, 1911, p 27.
4 EF Benson, *Queen Lucia*, London, 1920, p 18.
5 EW Gregory, *The Art and Craft of Home Making*, London, 1913, p 42.
6 JH Elder-Duncan, *The House Beautiful and Useful*, London 1911, p 140.
7 John Galsworthy, *A Modern Comedy*, London 1970 (1st published 1929), p 7.
8 G Whiteley Ward, *Common Commodities and Industries. Wallpaper*, 1921, p 72.

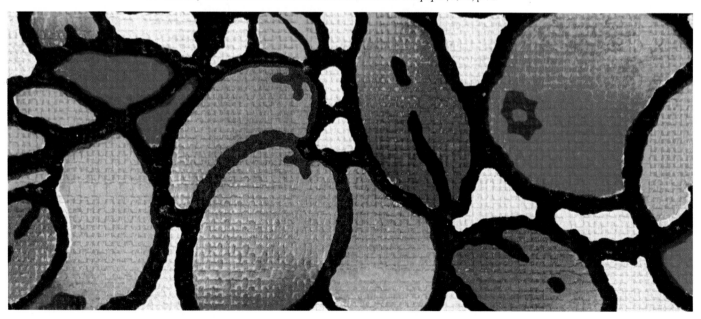

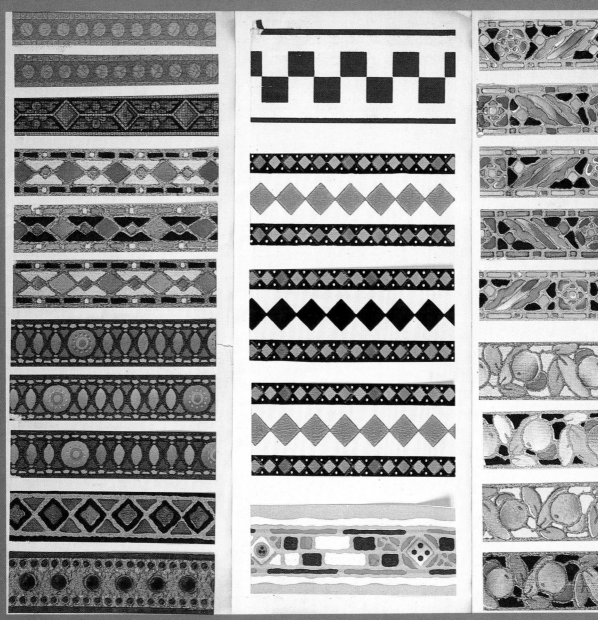

18, Right: Design for a chintz, 1912. All-over patterns of this sort were known in the trade as 'verdure'. The native flowers and foliage of this design would have fitted in beautifully with a traditional English decorative scheme.

19, Far right: Design for a printed textile using eighteenth-century motifs. 1912.

30 W x 20 h

447.

20, Above: Design for printed textile, 1913. Traditional chinoiserie designs with exotic birds and flowering trees were popular right through the first two decades of this century.

21 Design for chintz, 1910.

2379

22 'Futurist' design of the early 1920s.

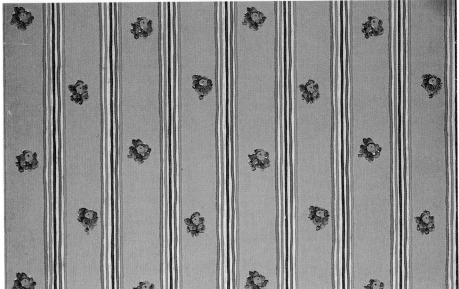

23, Left: Wallpaper, probably French, c 1920.

24, Far left: This textile design of the early 1920s employs a number of avant-garde motifs and colours but is not too aggressively 'futurist'.

25 Modern chinoiserie wallpaper in the
bright colours of the early 1920s.

26 Design for printed textile, 1919.

27 Cretonne designed by the Silver Studio in
1925. This 'Queen-Anne' design, with its
imitation stitchwork, would have gone well
with eighteenth-century furniture.

28, *Right:* The rich colours and dark ground
of this printed linen were typical of the mid-
1920s.

PART·FoUR:1925-1940

A·DIVISION·OF TASTES

Perhaps the most significant aspect of home decoration in the late 1920s and 30s was the ever widening gulf that existed between lower and upper middle-class taste. The work of the Silver Studio during this period shows this division with great clarity. Much of the studio's work was for firms with whom they had always dealt – Warner's, Liberty's, Sanderson and GP & J Baker. The textile designs they produced were often adaptations of late eighteenth-century and early nineteenth-century chintz patterns – baskets of flowers, exotic birds, rococo scrolls. Subsequently printed onto glazed cotton, these patterns epitomized the upper middle-class drawing-room of the 1930s and indeed remained popular for decades afterwards. A completely different sort of design was produced for the manufacturers of cheap furnishing textiles, linoleums and wallpapers. These were inspired by cubism, with their severe geometric forms softened by sprays of stylized flowers and leaves. Patterns of this type were enormously popular in working-class and lower middle-class houses throughout the 30s. Another notable feature of this period was the curious fact that the use of wallpaper was eschewed by anyone with pretentions to good taste, although it was the upper middle class who had spent such large sums of money on wallpaper in the late nineteenth and early twentieth centuries. Probably it was felt that patterned wallpaper was inappropriate as a background to eighteenth-century furniture, and that enough visual interest was supplied by furnishing textiles alone.

By the late 1920s an ever-increasing number of people were in a position to buy a small house of their own. Despite the Depression, there was a sharp expansion of service industries, particularly in London. Thus people from comparatively humble backgrounds found that they could afford the modest mortgage repayments on a new three-bedroomed semi-detached house on one of the thousands of housing estates which were springing up on the outskirts of every major English town. It became a popular weekend pastime for young couples to tour these estates in search of the perfect house at the right price. Even in London this could be less than £500, well within the range of a bank clerk or a skilled manual worker. Many of these houses had considerable charm. Although based on a traditional London terraced house plan, they often had low ceilings, picture and dado rails and French windows onto a fair sized garden. Externally, homely vernacular features were employed, such as tile hanging, half-timbering and roughcast. A cottage-like appearance was thought particularly desirable, so windows were often small-paned casements, and a tile-roofed porch was ubiquitous. In style these houses tended towards Jacobean rather than the more austere eighteenth-century styles. Most of the purchasers of these houses had come from inner suburban terraced houses, which if not actually Georgian, were often vaguely classical in style. They wanted a house which was as different as possible from the one they were leaving. In any case, local authority housing estates were often in a neo-Georgian style and this particularly insecure class of

1, Preceding pages: Modernist cut-out wallpaper corner, 1938.

2 An example of 'cottage' wallpaper from the late 1920s. This charming, inexpensive paper was usually either self-coloured or had a simple pattern of stripes and was invariably accompanied by a brightly coloured floral border. It was much used in less well-off houses.

3 Cheap tapestry wallpaper of the late 1920s. These richly coloured and densely patterned papers were a popular choice for the parlours and dining-rooms of small houses in the late 1920s and early 30s.

society did not want to live in a house that might be mistaken for one built by the council.

It was generally felt that if these houses bore a more than passing resemblance to a Tudor cottage on the outside, then the interior should follow suit. Naturally this meant that the predominant wood used for furniture should be oak. It was indeed the first time since the seventeenth century that this wood was popular for furnishing. The two previous centuries had been dominated by mahogany. Often a limited purse meant that the use of oak on furniture was confined to a thin veneer, and it was rare for the massiveness of Jacobean furniture to be imitated. Instead, High Street furnishing stores such as Times and Drages were full of spindly sideboards with barley sugar twist legs, and matching tables and chairs, all hopefully labelled Jacobean.

Much as the purchasers of these houses might despise their parents' Victorian furnishing and decoration, they adopted an approach to home decoration that was still very much part of the nineteenth century. There was no fear of strong colour combinations: green and orange, brown and yellow were boldly juxtaposed; and oak graining, a traditional decoration for both the exterior and interior of houses, was very widely used.

I mentioned earlier that small speculatively-built houses adhered to a traditional plan. The hall, always narrow, ran from the front door to the rear scullery with a staircase rising on one side. Off the other side would be the drawing-room (usually at the front of the house) and a dining-room with French windows on to a small paved terrace. As well as two or three bedrooms upstairs, there would be a bathroom. A not inconsiderable part of the attraction of this type of house was the inclusion of such modern features as electric lighting and constant hot water. Many of the new householders were used to gas lighting and cooking on coal-fired ranges and were quick to appreciate the saving in time and effort. Unlike the more prosperous middle classes, these people had no journals to advise on home decoration. The main inspiration for decorative schemes tended to come from showroom displays and a traditionally acquired taste – hence the juxtaposition of Modernist wallpaper and oak graining.

There tended to be a remarkable consistency about how these houses were decorated and furnished. The hall was invariably given both picture and dado rails, the dado traditionally being formed from anaglypta. Graining was the most popular form of treatment for the woodwork – light or dark oak being usual. In less well-off houses, or in those erected by the cheaper builders, the woodwork would be painted a deep chocolate brown, or chestnut (dried blood as it was often called). Varnished wallpapers were still very popular, as they had been fifty years earlier, but increasingly in the 30s an all-over leaf and berry pattern would be chosen, or a cubist paper in much-favoured autumn tints (namely orange, brown, cream and green). Sometimes a plain embossed paper in biscuit would be used, with a brightly

4 A typical lower middle-class interior of the 1930s, with dark brown varnished woodwork.

5 An upper middle-class bedroom of the late 1920s in which light colours are combined with antique furniture of the late eighteenth and early nineteenth centuries.

coloured frieze below the picture rail. The hall and landing floors were usually covered in a brown linoleum, sometimes patterned to resemble parquet flooring. A narrow strip of stair-carpet was usual, often with a pattern which vaguely matched the wallpaper. There was not much room for furniture. A Jacobean oak hall wardrobe was popular and perhaps a small table. A few popular prints might hang from the walls or poor-quality watercolours of Highland or Lake District scenes. Invariably the overall effect would be one of considerable varnished gloom, dimly lit at night by a low-wattage light bulb in a lantern shade.

The drawing-room of these houses tended to be kept for weekend use and for important occasions. Money was often in very short supply and constantly heating two rooms was not practicable. If light colours were used at all, it was in this room. Particularly in the late 20s an imitation silk moiré wallpaper in pale pink, yellow or green might be used, with a floral border below the picture rail. Increasingly in the 30s, a plain biscuit-coloured paper was used, with either a flower or cubist border. During the 30s, borders became more elaborate, with cut-out corners to form large panels on the wall. Some firms, like John Line, devised decorative friezes to go above the skirting board in the form of herbaceous borders. A sofa and at least two armchairs were usual. These would be given loose covers of cretonne, often in a neo-Jacobean pattern. Glazed chintz was not as popular as in the upper middle-class house as it was felt to be too Victorian. There would be a china cabinet for displaying wedding presents and usually an upright piano. Linoleum was often used as a border for a carpet square, which might be a traditional Axminster or Brussels, perhaps in the late 30s enlivened by a few cubist rugs. In better-off houses the curtains might be of velvet in this room, but thin unlined cotton or cotton and rayon mixture was very much more usual. Often the curtains would be of the same pattern throughout the house to give a uniform appearance from the outside. Sometimes nineteenth-century oil or watercolour landscape paintings had been inherited and it was in this room that these would be displayed.

The dining-room was the most charming room in these houses. Frequently a fire was kept burning throughout the day, as this was the fire that had a back boiler for the domestic hot water supply. As a consequence this was the room that was in constant use. Here would be the wireless, and the dining-room table could be used for homework and reading when not in use for meals. The furniture was nearly always Jacobean in style, though a large Victorian sideboard might have been inherited. There would be a dining table and six chairs, usually an armchair or two, the sideboard and often a bureau and bookcase. Invariably this room was lit by an overhead imitation alabaster bowl lamp, suspended by chains from the ceiling. Like the hall, an anaglypta dado was common in this room and would be given the same oak graining. Because of a constant coal fire, the wallpaper was frequently changed, and in the 30s this room was most likely to have a

6 & 7 Two examples of 'sanitary' wallpapers from circa 1930. These were often sold ready varnished for use in kitchens and bathrooms and for dadoes which received a lot of wear, such as those in halls and dining-rooms.

Modernist paper. Linoleum was invariably used, often in an imitation Turkey carpet pattern, but there would be lots of small rugs here too, often home-made. (Rug-making was a popular pastime in the 30s.)

Kitchens and bathrooms in these houses were nearly always painted in either gloss or matt oil paint, chosen from a limited colour range. Again, this was a nineteenth-century practice that had continued. Typical colours were sage or eau-de-nil green, cream and hedge-sparrow blue. The kitchen would often have a built-in dresser with glass doors and cupboards below. There would be a deep white porcelain sink and a few shelves. In better houses both bathroom and kitchen would be tiled to dado height and in some instances the kitchen would have an Ideal coke boiler for hot water.

Bedrooms in these houses were often depositories for parental cast-off Victorian furniture. (Indeed, I have seen several untouched houses of this period where neglected eighteenth-century chests of drawers had been in unappreciated use.) A new veneered walnut bedroom suite from Drages might be the ideal, but more often than not, the bedrooms were filled with large slabs of mahogany dating from the 1880s and 90s, in the form of wardrobes, dressing tables, chests of drawers and wash-stands that more prosperous relations were glad to dispose of. Polished linoleum, often in a floral pattern, was the usual floor covering, with mats placed in strategic positions. Modernist wallpapers were not much used in bedrooms, instead pretty sprigged chintz designs were popular as was plain distemper. Here too the woodwork might well be ivory or cream, instead of brown.

The contrast with the upper middle-class house could not have been greater. The ideal interior to be achieved here was that of a late eighteenth-century manor house, even though it might well have to be done in a new house in Hampstead Garden Suburb or Metropolitan Buckinghamshire. Since the early 1900s this section of society had been copiously supplied with photographs of the interiors of such houses, initially through the pages of *Country Life* and during the 20s and 30s through the home-decorating magazines such as *House & Garden* and *Ideal Homes.*

During the late 20s and throughout the 30s a large number of the professional classes were able to achieve something approaching pre-war prosperity. Comparatively large sums of money were still to be made in stockbroking, banking and the legal profession and in London at least many businessmen prospered. It was in the Home Counties that large quantities of substantial houses in an acre or two of garden were erected. Tudorbethan was still a great favourite but unlike speculatively-built houses, neo-Georgian was very popular too.

The owners of these houses were often of sound nineteenth-century professional stock, well-educated and much interested in all aspects of house decoration. Thirty or forty years earlier it was this class of society that had led the way in changing attitudes to home decorating. Vast sums had been lavished on hand-blocked wallpapers and silk upholstery to achieve hugely

8 Sanitary damask paper with matching cut-out border. Sometimes a varnished sanitary paper was used in dining-rooms. This example dates from around 1930, although this pattern was available from the 1890s onwards.

9 An upper middle-class dining-room of the late 1920s. Note the plain walls and the combination of antique furniture and Persian rugs.

cluttered interiors. Since then a great thinning-out process had taken place; a decorating style evolved which became the accepted manner among the upper middle classes and which is still to be recognized as such in drawing-rooms today. It is characterized by plain, light colour schemes and homely pieces of antique furniture mixed with Oriental rugs and glazed chintz. While its general character may be described as neo-Georgian, it is by no means rigidly historical. 'Taste', it was felt, existed in the right selection of different items in the same room and not in the creation of historically accurate 'period' rooms. Thus R Randal Phillips wrote in 'The Modern English Interior' (*Country Life* 1928):

> 'The "period" room is certainly to be discredited, for it is no more than a dull, dead repetition of a past time totally unconnected with the present ... '

It was to be distinguished from the room of eighteenth-century inspiration, which along with Old English and Modernistic was one of the main decorating styles of the 20s and 30s:

> ' ... a sitting room in more formal style, with refinement in all its details: say, a room with panelled walls painted parchment colour, sash windows hung with gaily patterned chintz, walnut or mahogany furniture displaying a fine sense of design and the art of the cabinetmaker, a floor of low-toned oak boards overspread with Persian rugs ... '

10 Design for a printed furnishing linen in a Jacobean style, 1936. Designs such as this were – and still are – very popular for rooms with dark oak furniture.

Emulating as always the aristocracy, the upper middle classes attached great importance to a spacious entrance hall. It would often contain a chimney piece so that it could be used as a species of sitting-room. Frequently this room would be panelled either in oak, if the style of the house was Tudor, or painted if it was neo-Georgian. The floor was nearly always of polished oak and liberally scattered with Persian Tribal rugs. Tribal rugs were easily available at comparatively little cost between the wars. Most large London stores had a section devoted to their sale, Liberty's being (and still is) the most famous. An eighteenth- or early nineteenth-century grandfather clock was *de rigueur* and there might well be a good eighteenth-century chest of drawers or seventeenth-century oak blanket chest. There was no need for hat stands in these houses. A capacious cloakroom and gentlemen's lavatory invariably led off the hall. Here were stored old mackintoshes, croquet mallets, gum boots and bound volumes of *Punch*. The hall and staircase walls might well be hung with sporting prints and old engravings.

The drawing-room of these houses would also sport at least one and often two or more pairs of French windows leading onto a paved or gravel terrace. Like the hall, the floor would be of polished wood, scattered with rugs. This room would be in constant use. Here would be the best pieces of antique furniture – a walnut tallboy, several good chests of drawers, perhaps a small bureau. Comfortable sofas and armchairs would be covered in glazed chintz in a variety of reproduction eighteenth-century patterns. On the walls would be good engravings, old English watercolours, perhaps some silhouettes and miniatures. Although there might be a chandelier, it was usual in these houses to light a room by expensively shaded table lamps and ormolu wall sconces, so that in the evenings there would be pools of light and no harsh overhead glare. No wallpaper was used, except perhaps in servants' bedrooms. No grained paint would be found, unless it was used for kitchen cupboards. A comparatively light distemper would normally be chosen. (The poor used distemper because it was cheap, the rich used it for the subtle effects that could be obtained.) Sometimes matt oil paint was used for rooms that received a lot of wear, such as halls and dining-rooms. Typical drawing-room colours were eau-de-nil or sage green, cream, stone or primrose yellow. Woodwork was often in the same colour as the walls, or another light colour, cream and ivory being particularly popular. White, however, was very rarely used. Strong colours in the drawing-room were provided by the Persian rugs and the chintzes, which might well have a rich red or maroon ground.

Dining-rooms tended to be either distinctly cottagey in character with gate-leg tables, Welsh dressers and quantities of Staffordshire china figures and transfer-printed plates, or more formal and Georgian, with a late eighteenth-century mahogany dining table and sideboard. Here would be hung portraits of real or purchased ancestors, and the sideboard would often display a quantity of well-polished plate. If no library or study existed there would almost certainly be a desk or bureau in this room, and real Turkey carpets on the floor. Although deep red was still a popular dining-room colour in the 1920s, it was gradually being superseded by lighter colours, such as apple green and pale blue. Like the drawing-room, wall sconces and lamps were often used for lighting.

If the small suburban house bedroom was a rather bleak affair, quite the reverse was the case for important bedrooms in the upper middle-class home. The main bedroom and best spare room were invariably furnished with antiques, usually eighteenth-century country pieces. The beds might be antique too, but were more often something modern and useful from Heal's. More silk-shaded lamps and Persian rugs would be in evidence and glazed chintzes were popular for bedspreads and curtains. The main bedroom might well contain an armchair and sofa. No gentleman's house was

11 A typical prosperous middle-class
entrance hall of the 30s. Spacious, filled with
antique furniture and the plain walls hung
with old prints and watercolours.

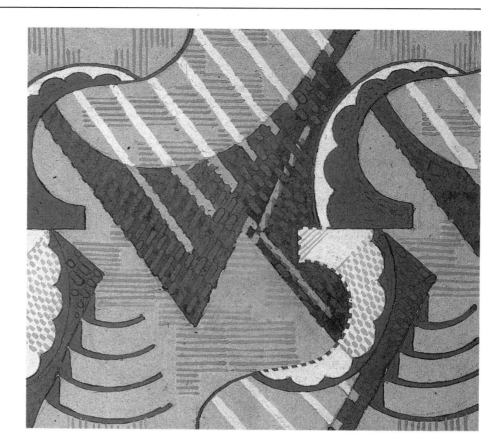

12 Design for a Modernist carpet by John Churton of the Silver Studio, 1933.

13, Right: Design for modernist printed textile, 1932.

complete without a dressing room, filled with eighteenth-century wardrobe, chest of drawers and quantities of silver or ivory hair brushes, and endless family photographs in leather frames.

During the 1930s, the Silver Studio produced many hundreds of designs for textiles and wallpapers in a style which was then known as 'Modernist'. These patterns consisted largely of geometric shapes distantly echoing the forms of cubist paintings and reflecting the decorative modernism which emanated from France in the 20s. While often thought of as typifying the inter-war period, this style was reviled by most educated commentators as a nightmare of vulgarity redolent of the cinema and the bypass factory. It enjoyed popularity above all in the small suburban house on cheaper items such as china, wallpaper and rugs, with the strident colours of 'Art Deco' muted into autumnal browns and orange. For more substantial purchases of furniture, a reproduction historical style would usually still be chosen. Critics found the juxtaposition of cheaply fashionable patterns with Jacobean furniture deeply objectionable. Paul Nash wrote in *Room and Book* in 1932:

'Someone in an unhappy moment invented the word "modernistic" … the Jazz repp cushion, in the sham Jacobean chair, the "abstract" rug from the Tottenham Court Road dozing by the brick hearth.'

Although Art Deco modernism enjoyed a measure of popularity, the Modern Movement itself made little impact on middle-class taste in the 1930s. There were however a number of other developments in interior decoration between the wars which deserve mention here.

A conspicuous tendency of decorative fashion in the 1920s was to react against excessive refinement and 'taste' in decoration and furnishing. This often took the form of a revival of what then seemed the more *outré* historical styles, though rarely in a form that did the original much justice. Though often calculated to outrage conventional taste, such trends are of interest in this context because what had been the province of a sophisticated minority between the wars became influential in shaping middle-class taste after the Second World War.

One of the more readily assimilated styles was what Osbert Lancaster termed 'Curzon Street Baroque'. Inspired by Sacheverell Sitwell's *Southern Baroque Art* of 1924, fashionable aesthetes sought out gilded figures of angels, cherubs and saints with which to adorn their Mayfair apartments. Walls were roughly distempered in warm Mediterranean colours and quantities of wrought-iron and contorted oak furniture imported. All this found an odd echo in the suburbs in the architectural style labelled 'Pseudish' in Lancaster's terminology. White-painted walls, coloured pantiles and wrought-ironwork became conspicuous in the new suburbs, housing distempered rooms of ornate furniture, Spanish leather and liberal amounts of gilding. The suburbanite's enthusiasm for the Mediterranean has not, of course, abated, fuelled since the Second World War by the advent of cheap foreign holidays and still influencing the appearance of suburban homes.

Another trend of the 20s whose frequent excesses were satirized by Osbert Lancaster was 'Vogue Regency'. Before 1914, the 'debased' Regency style had been admired by only a handful of connoisseurs and architects, among them AE Richardson, Gerald Wellesley and Edward Knoblock. At his houses in London and Worthing, Knoblock recreated Regency decorative schemes to house his collection of black-and-gold Thomas Hope furniture. In the 20s these became well known. Knoblock exhibited his furniture at the 1924 British Empire Exhibition at Wembley in an '1815 Room' designed by AE Richardson and it even found its way into *Good Housekeeping*. Regency furniture began to appear in many fasionable drawing-rooms, though rarely in so sympathetic a setting as that created by Knoblock. One of its supposed virtues was that it 'went well' with modern furniture; Vogue Regency was thus a curious combination of rather sparse antiques with stark Modernist pieces, with perhaps a dash of Curzon Street Baroque for good measure. The total effect owed far more to the 1920s than the 1820s. Vogue Regency enjoyed an equally modish after-life in the 1950s, when Regency striped wallpapers were enthusiastically rediscovered and employed in conjunction with white-painted woodwork and antique and 'contemporary' furniture.

An aspect of taste in the 20s and 30s of more lasting importance was the

14 Modernist pattern wallpaper, 1934.

15 Modernist pattern wallpaper, 1934. It was usual in the 1930s to soften cubist patterns with sprays of leaves and flowers.

16 A smart interior of the late 1930s, an example of 'Vogue Regency' in which one or two early nineteenth-century pieces are combined with antique furniture of earlier periods and fitted carpets.

revival of interest in the arts of the early and mid-Victorian periods. As early as 1919, in his essay 'The Ottoman and the Whatnot', Roger Fry noted – with disdain, naturally – the reappearance of 'Victoriana' in London drawing-rooms. Alongside the '1815 Room' at the 1924 Wembley Exhibition was one of '1852' designed by the architect and scholar HS Goodhart-Rendel, who did perhaps more than anyone in these years to correct misapprehensions about Victorian architecture. And that same year at Oxford a group of undergraduate aesthetes, among them Harold Acton, Robert Byron and Evelyn Waugh, planned an '1840 Exhibition' to display their collections of early Victorian *objets d'art*: glass domes containing wax flowers and fruit, millefiori paperweights, woolwork pictures, Staffordshire china and mahogany furniture. In the event the exhibition never took place but the seeds of a Victorian revival were sown. As Harold Acton noted, it 'had left its mark on local fashion and interior decoration' and by the late 20s 'Victoriana' was being assiduously collected.

While such trends ran against the aesthetic dogmas of Roger Fry and, later, Nikolaus Pevsner, they found a creative response among designers seeking an alternative to the Modern Movement. It was a peculiarly English response, returning to tradition for inspiration and accompanying perhaps a wider recognition that many English traditions were on the point of dying.

Perhaps most immediately relevant to domestic furnishing were the textiles produced by a small number of enlightened manufacturers. Improved developments in screen-printing techniques enabled manufacturers to produce experimental textiles in a manner which would hitherto have been uneconomic. Morton Sundour, Donald Bros, the Old Bleach Linen Co, and above all Allan and Roger Walton produced superb work by talented designers. Donald Bros employed Marion Dorn; Allan Walton commissioned a large number of artists and designers, including Duncan Grant, Vanessa Bell and Frank Dobson. Similarly a few manufacturers of woven textiles, among them Morton Sundour, who owned the Edinburgh Weavers, Donald Bros' famous *Old Glamis* fabrics and Warner & Sons Ltd, were anxious to employ the best designers of the decade. The Silver Studio produced a large number of designs for textiles in this vein for Warners, Donald Bros and Morton Sundour, as well as providing more faithful copies of Regency chintzes.

Due to the unpopularity of wallpaper among the educated middle classes in this period there was little produced which fits into this category. However, the artist Edward Bawden was inspired by a William Morris wallpaper seen at another of the period rooms at the 1924 Wembley exhibition to begin making his own designs. The results were lithographically printed by the Curwen Press and marketed by Modern Textiles in a brave attempt to reintroduce wallpaper into the middle-class home. The first batch of designs of 1926 were highly pictorial and had a strong flavour of nineteenth-century popular art about them; the *Mermaid* design, for instance, indicates the growing appreciation of the charms of popular English seaside art. Abandoning the drop repeat format of most mass-produced wallpaper, Bawden used a single repeatable unit which usually consisted of a small vignette surrounded by a decorative border, a device owing more to nineteenth-century transfer prints and engravings than to William Morris. In addition, Cole and Sons produced some delightful designs by John Aldridge which were inspired by early nineteenth-century lining papers and sprigged muslins.

In the field of ceramics, the designs for Wedgwood made by Eric Ravilious, a friend of Bawden's, were inspired by nineteenth-century transfer ware and are among the most engaging productions of the 1930s.

Just as the intellectual middle class was learning to appreciate traditional English popular art, so authentic country-cottage interiors began to disappear. The contents of cottage dressers – usually laden with lustre jugs and Staffordshire figures – were being eagerly bought by antique dealers. The cottages themselves were often acquired by the middle class for modernization – a process which has rapidly accelerated since the war.

In a similar way, authentic 1930s' interiors are rapidly disappearing. This is a great pity, as it is our last opportunity to glimpse what life was like before the Second World War, when coal was still the main form of domestic heating, and richly coloured linoleum the most common form of floor-covering. We hope that a house of this period can be preserved, so that future generations can see what is now fast becoming a vanished way of life.

17 Interior of a cottage at Crewkerne, Somerset by Edwin Smith. Here we can see a typical late 1920s cheap wallpaper *in situ*.
145

18, Above & right: Two examples of 'cottage' wallpapers from the late 1920s (see illustration 2).

19, 20 & 21 Three examples of richly coloured and exotic wallpapers which first became fashionable in the early 1920s and were still popular ten years later.

22 & 23 Two examples of characteristic tapestry papers of the 1930s. These all-over leaf designs were as popular in the 1930s as they were in the 20s but in predominately brown and orange colours.

24, Right: Design for a wallpaper, 1933.

10½"w × 16½"h.

2Cols.

1 2 3 4 5 6.

2 Blotch.

{ Plane
  Beech.

7015.

25 Cut-out wallpaper decoration, 1938. Wallpaper borders and cut-out decorations became increasingly elaborate in the 1930s.

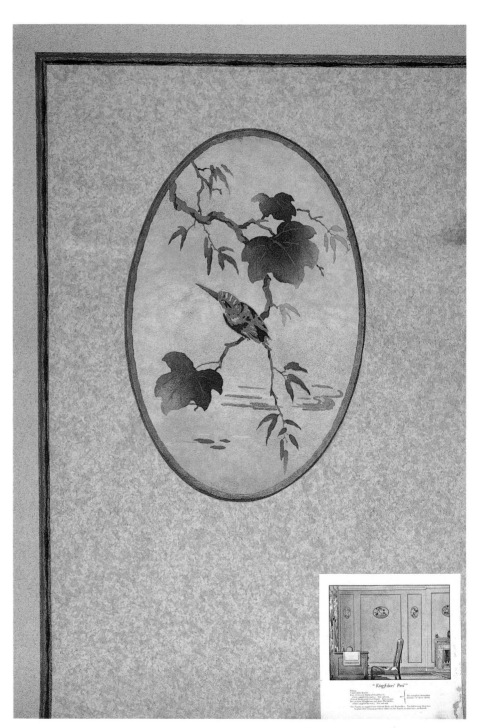

26, Far right, above: Neo-Adam chintz design by Frank Price of the Silver Studio, 1940.

27, Far right, below: Late eighteenth-century revival chintz pattern by Frank Price of the Silver Studio, 1938. This is typical of the patterns used by the more prosperous middle class in the late 1930s for loose covers and curtains. Such designs are still very popular today.

28 Design for a printed furnishing textile, 1934. This is an early example of the growing interest in English nineteenth-century popular art. The design is based on an early Victorian wallpaper, with sea shells testifying to an appreciation of the English seaside.

PRACTICAL · SUGGESTIONS

There are now several guides to the authentic restoration (both inside and out) of the nineteenth-century small house. Particularly useful is *Putting Back the Style*, edited by Alexandra Artley (Evans Bros Ltd, 1982). It also gives advice for owners of smarter houses and flats of the early twentieth century, but does not cover small surburban houses of the 1920s and 30s. Americans are especially fortunate in being able to subscribe to *The Old House Journal*, which is devoted to restoration, maintenance and decoration of modest pre-1939 houses and is very good indeed.

Fortunately suitable wallpapers and textiles for small nineteenth century houses are fairly easy to obtain and need not be expensive. A good range will be available from the Silver Studio Collection which is part of a project to licence Silver Studio designs. The designs will not only be on wallpapers and furnishing textiles but also used as an inspiration for bed-linen, lighting, and a wide range of small decorative objects.

Sadly it is at present impossible to buy typical wallpapers of the 1920s and 30s. It is hoped that this is a situation that will presently change as more wallpaper designs from the Silver Studio are made available over the next few years.

Here are a few general hints to owners of houses who want to preserve the character of their property and who want to decorate in a style appropriate to the period. Specific advice on colours and patterns are already given in the preceding chapters.

EXTERIORS
1. Windows
Windows are one of the most important visual elements in the exterior of the house. Not only the shape of the openings, but the number and proportion of the panes, the moulding of the frames and the spacing and moulding of the glazing bars are fundamental in deciding the appearance of the house, and all would have been carefully considered by the builder. Furthermore, when seen from inside they can frame and enhance a view that may otherwise leave something to be desired. The replacement of windows should therefore be undertaken with extreme caution if the architectural quality of the house is to be preserved. Usually, replacement is rarely necessary unless the frames have been allowed to deteriorate to a very great extent. The metal-framed windows that were so common on inter-war houses are an exception to this. They are now showing signs of deterioration

which are beyond hope of repair. It is never wise to fit highly expensive aluminium or PVC-clad double glazing. As Amercans have already discovered to their cost, aluminium windows can deteriorate far more quickly than properly painted wood or steel ones, as well as ruining the character of one's house. If for insulation or sound-proofing purposes double glazing is deemed desirable, then it is much more satisfactory to fit secondary windows.

The painting of windows is particularly important. Now that the fashion for white paint is almost universal, it is difficult to imagine how richly coloured the exteriors of houses once were. Throughout the nineteenth century, the most common colours for exterior woodwork were grey, cream, black or chocolate. Various shades of dark green or red were also frequently seen, but were slightly more expensive. Another treatment for external wood work was to brush-grain it. This involved painting the woodwork cream and then overpainting with a coloured turpentine mixture; or with beer and water, which was then patterned to imitate wood and subsequently varnished. From the 1890s, ready-mixed graining paint became available and one could choose from a whole range of wood colours, various shades of oak being by far the most popular. Grained exterior woodwork remained quite usual until the 1940s. These ready-mixed graining paints are still available today from larger decorator's merchants. Another popular and traditional treatment, particularly suitable for casement windows, is to use two contrasting colours. The outer frame in one and the opening parts in another. Chocolate brown and pale yellow, dark green and cream, Indian red and cream and pale green and buff were all highly popular. It was a way of making one's house distinctive without spoiling the unity of the terrace of houses. Stone lintels and window sills were always left unpainted. If one has painted lintels and sills, then use cream or buff. Metal windows in the 1930s were invariably painted in a shade of brown, dark green or Venetian red, never white.

2. Walls

If your house is built of unadorned brick, it is important that any repointing is done with great care. If, however, you own a house built in the 1920s or 30s, there is a strong possibility that the walls are covered with pebble dash or cement rendering. Pebble dash was not intended to be painted but this is now the universal practice. Cream looks more authentic than dead white if you are repainting. On a 30s modernist home, white was the usual shade for the rendering.

3. Doors

A current, regrettably widespread fashion is for replacing front doors with period designs made from tropical hardwoods, cheaply imported from the disappearing rain forests of South America and the Far East. These are

THE BOOK
: OF THE :
HOME

A typical middle-class drawing-room circa 1890.

inappropriate in both style and material. If your house has its original front door, then every effort should be made to keep it. If you are stuck with a bad modern one, a demolition yard may provide a suitable replacement, or have one made. Some of the large joinery manufacturers make a good range of traditional doors suitable for many houses of the period 1880-1940. Check with neighbouring houses to find the correct style if in any doubt.

INTERIORS

Until the late 1950s, the appearance of modest houses changed very little, both inside and out. However, growing affluence and a desire to be 'modern' led to drastic alterations being made, particularly to the interiors. This has entailed the ruthless removal of fixtures such as chimneypieces, cast-iron baths and built-in cupboards and kitchen dressers. Dining-rooms and sitting-rooms have often been knocked into one large room, destroying the proportions of both. A particularly dreary obsession that began in the late 1950s is the belief that wooden and plaster mouldings trap dust. This has led to panelled doors being covered in hardboard and the removal of picture and dado rails. Deep moulded wainscot has often been replaced by a mean, narrow strip of skirting. For owners of houses of the period, or would-be purchasers, here are a few hints to bear in mind when doing up the interior.

1. Fireplaces

Fireplaces were the focal point of all major rooms in the houses of the period 1880-1940. Do try to retain open fires in sitting-rooms and dining-rooms. If the chimneypieces have been removed, try to discover from a neighbour what the correct style should be and act accordingly. Open fires not only look delightful but provide an excellent source of ventilation.

2. Joinery

It is now very easy to obtain the correct mouldings for picture and dado rails and for skirting boards. Picture rails were used in all the main rooms of most houses of the period covered by this book. Dado rails were often to be found in the hall and dining-room. Again, an inspection of a neighbour's house should reveal what type of mouldings were used and in which rooms. Panelled doors are also easily replaced. A good range of accurate reproduction doors of all periods is available from larger joinery manufacturers. Genuine ones can be found at demolition merchants.

3. Colour schemes

For the last thirty years or so, many people have refused to consider any colour but white for internal woodwork. For modest houses of the period 1880-1940, a rich, dark effect was nearly always preferred. Specific colours are mentioned in the appropriate chapters, but do try brush-graining some internal woodwork. It is not a difficult technique to learn, and it helps create a truly authentic effect, particularly in smaller houses.

4. Floor-coverings

For most of the period in question patterned linoleum or floor-cloth was the most common floor-covering. Although still available in the United States, it is no longer to be found in England, except on rubbish skips or in junk shops. However, good copies of late nineteenth-century Axminster carpets are still made, and large carpet squares of all periods turn up at auction sales.

From the 1890s onwards, a popular treatment was to stain and polish a floorboard surround for a large carpet square. Fitted carpets were never used in houses between 1890 and 1920.

5. Kitchens and bathrooms

Whilst not advocating an attempt to live in a room reminiscent of a museum, it is worth trying to keep as much of the original fixtures of kitchens and bathrooms as possible. As late as the 1930s, bathrooms were fitted with good-quality cast-iron baths and ceramic wash-basins. Similarly a solid wood dresser and tongue-and-groove panelled cupboards were common fittings in even the smallest kitchen. It makes much more sense to retain and restore the original fittings than to rip them out and replace them with expensive chipboard and formica.

INDEX

PICTURE CREDITS

Black & White
Beamish, North of England Open Air Museum *72*
Greater London Records Office *81*
Royal Commission on the Historical Monuments of England *70 (above), 82 (above), 26*
Southampton City Museums and Art Gallery *11, 35, 44 (above), 52 (above), 155*
Edwin Smith *144 (left)*

Colour
British Library *97, 103*
The Tate Gallery *36*